MW01172894

CONSCIENCES
OF AN
IMMIGRANT

Alexandre Telfort Fils

CONSCIENCES

—— OF AN ——

IMMIGRANT

PRO
EDITIONS

Novembre 2024, Publié par Pro Éditions
516, Delmas 66 (Route de Delmas), Port-au-Prince, Haïti
Tél. : (+509) 3121-5441 / 4750-4572 / 4166-3140
editions@correctpro.net
www.correctpro.net

CONSCIENCES OF AN IMMIGRANT

ISBN : 979-8-218-53238-3

Bibliothèque nationale d'Haïti
Couverture et mise en page par Pro Éditions
©Tous droits réservés
Alexandre Telfort Fils

CONTENTS

Preface 9

Preliminary Note 15

Foreword 17

Introduction 21

Chapter One 33

   Conscience of where we come from 33

Chapter Two 45

   Conscience that the act of migration is not dehumanizing 45

Chapter Three 61

   Conscience of the Challenges of Integration 61

Chapter four 79

   Conscience of political issues 79

Chapter Five... 89

   Conscience of the Double Consciousness 89

Chapter six 99

   Conscience of the challenges and richness of diversity 99

Chapter Seven 105

   Conscience that the American Dream doesn't belong to all of us...... 105

Chapter Eight 111

   Conscience of the future that is ours 111

   Conclusion 119

   Annex 1 129

   Annex 2 133

   Bibliography 143

PREFACE

When this young prodigy of Haitian politics, whose clarity and determination I admire so much, invited me to preface this book, *Consciences of an Immigrant,* I immediately felt challenged. It's an appeal to my own conscience, that of an immigrant grappling with the demands of a new world, where my choices have been dictated by the inexorable necessity of adapting to a country that is not my own.

Conscience is often described as our inner judge. For an immigrant, it becomes a compass that guides his awakening to another world. This awakening can open the way to new possibilities, as well as reveal realities harsher than those we had hoped to escape. Every immigrant in search of this often idealized "El Dorado" bears the scars of a homeland marked by shattered dreams and dashed hopes.

In this book, Alexandre Telfort Fils takes a daring gamble: to make the world resonate with the vibrations of a plurality of consciousness. And he succeeds brilliantly. The attentive and curious reader will be surprised, as I was, by the maturity that shines through both in his deep reflection and in the intensity of his convictions. Her powerful, rebellious cry, raised with all the strength of her being, echoes the silent struggles of those who suffer the injustices of immigration, giving voice to those who can only murmur muffled complaints.

In pages that can be devoured voraciously, the author awakens a new sensitivity in us, tracing not only his own journey, but that of thousands of immigrants from Haiti and elsewhere, whose stories are interwoven with those of the nations that welcome them. With sometimes sickening finesse, he dissects the many facets of migration, reminding us that the immigrant is not simply a refugee from his or her homeland. He becomes the mirror of a collective consciousness, that of a community that, despite the storms of life, continues to believe in a better future. Leaving behind his roots, his culture, and sometimes even an intimate part of his identity, he never renounces his humanity. Every step he takes bears the visible or invisible scars of the torments he has endured and the calamities he has overcome. In this painful journey, he strives to reinvent himself, relentlessly seeking a new, hopeful destiny despite the obstacles that stand in the way of his integration and success.

Consciences of an Immigrant is more than a simple account of events; it's a profound reflection on the condition of immigrants and their quest to integrate into societies that are sometimes hostile or difficult to reach. This book also evokes the cultural richness that these millions of travelers bring, in spite of themselves, to their host countries. By opening their doors to souls in search of survival, these nations sometimes forge a clear conscience, even an extra measure of humanity. The work of this young leader, however, invites us to go beyond this simplistic vision. It encourages us to broaden our perspective, to see the immigrant not as a threat or a burden, but as an essential player in collective progress. By encouraging us to rethink our place in this dynamic, it challenges us to envision a future in which every voice and every story is not only recognized but valued for its legitimacy and power.

This book also paves the way for an intergenerational dialogue that questions what it means to be Haitian in the United States of America today. It proposes perspectives for a more inclusive society, where integration does not dilute identities, but enriches and sublimates them, strengthening the social fabric in all its rich diversity.

Alexandre Telfort Fils recognizes that we live in a time when immigration is at the center of passionate, polarizing debates that often reduce immigrants to mere numbers and statistics, dehumanizing lives rich with dreams and aspirations. In writing this book, the author seeks to show that behind every immigrant is a unique story, often rooted in complex political, economic, and social contexts that are too often overshadowed and now deserve to be heard and understood.

The American political landscape is currently in a state of flux, with the immigration debate fraught with strong emotions and profound contradictions. This country, built on successive waves of immigrants, seems to be wavering on how to deal with this crucial issue. On the one hand, America is glorified as a land of welcome; on the other, there is a growing fear of the foreigner, fueled by controversial political rhetoric. As an immigrant, the author has experienced these contradictions firsthand. Although often portrayed as essential to the economy and cultural diversity, immigrants also face restrictive policies and hostile rhetoric. This book was born out of that frustration, the feeling of being trapped between two contradictory narratives. The author wants to show that immigration is not a problem to be solved, but a reality to be understood, a richness to be embraced. Yes, there are legitimate challenges to integration and economic impact, but these issues must not obscure the essential point: immigration is above all a human story, rich in experiences and aspirations that should be valued and exploited to the full.

Through his reflections and encounters, the author questions our common humanity. What makes us reject others? Why is it so difficult to welcome the other as a source of mutual enrichment? Through his experiences, he shows that we all have something to gain from opening our minds and hearts. The real danger for society is not the arrival of newcomers, but withdrawal, fear of the other, and forgetting our fundamental values.

Conscience of an Immigrant is a call to this collective consciousness, to this ability to see beyond appearances and recognize the humanity of others. As an immigrant, the author had to leave not only a territory but also a life, a history, a part of himself with prestigious status and responsibilities, having been an advisor to the president and president of a political party in his home country. What was supposed to be a simple stopover turned into a prolonged exile, a forced stay that further complicated his dilemma and intensified his desire to return. Like so many others, he is forced to reinvent himself, rebuild his life, and contribute, often reluctantly but with great generosity, to the progress of his host country, while his homeland continues to crumble under the weight of all its misfortunes. Such stories underscore the urgent need to reform migration policies, not only to facilitate the integration of immigrants, but also to address the root causes of forced displacement, so that exile is no longer the only option for those seeking to build a dignified future for themselves and their country.

It is also an appeal to their immigrant brothers and sisters, urging them to become aware of their conditions and to stand up against the prejudice and hate speech that plague the often-over-politicized debate on immigration. Offering a perspective that is both intimate and universal, this book raises fundamental questions about our ability to respect the dignity of every individual, regardless of their background. It reminds us that it's time to change the narrative. We are much more than numbers or residence permits; we are human beings, bearers of dreams and hopes. In this sense, this book is an essential contribution to this transformation, an act of resistance against indifference, an act of faith in the future, and a declaration of love for this country that, despite its imperfections, offers the opportunity to live, to flourish and to actively contribute to collective development.

The challenges of a migratory journey should not be seen as insurmountable obstacles but as testimonies of resilience and courage. Beyond our individuality, it's crucial to recognize that integration is a shared challenge. This book aims to highlight the stories of those who, like me, are struggling to integrate while preserving their identities.

Armed with this conviction, the author shows, through his own situation, that immigration is much more than a simple geographical displacement; it is an intimate journey into the depths of one's conscience, questioning certainties, choices and even values once thought unassailable. This testimony is more than a personal account; it is a political plea for dignity and justice for all those who, like him, are forced to leave their country to escape instability and insecurity.

By recounting his journey, he aims to give voice to voices that are often ignored, to demystify the experience of migration, and to question a system that, despite its ideals of freedom and equality, sometimes seems to forget these fundamental values when faced with those who legitimately seek refuge, driven to the depths of their souls by the hope of a better life.

Alexandre Telfort Fils proudly tells the unique story of Haitian immigrants, whose journey to the United States is a story marked by the blood, sweat, and sacrifice of our ancestors. This journey is honored by the exemplary courage of those who fought in one of the bloodiest battles of the American Revolution: the Battle of Savannah, Georgia, between September and October 1779. It is also marked by the vision of a man from Saint-Marc who crossed the continent to found one of the greatest and most beautiful cities in America. It is imbued with the dignity of workers from all walks of life, be they creators, inventors, or designers.

It sheds new light on the epic of 1804, when Haiti did more than become the first free black republic in the modern world. It became the beacon of a new order, proclaiming loud and clear the dignity of all human beings, regardless of race or social background. In this epic moment, Haiti not only broke the chains of oppression, but embodied the hope of universal freedom, a freedom that centuries of colonization and injustice had long denied to so many souls. It was not just a revolution, but the breath of a collective conscience, heralding a world in which equality would be the right of all. Like a shock wave, his revolution reverberated around the globe, inspiring the struggles for freedom and justice that were to follow, and marking the beginning of a new world in which freedom was no longer a privilege, but the inalienable right of every human being. This historic turning point also had an unexpected impact on Louisiana and played a pivotal role in its destiny. As Napoleon Bonaparte sought to rebuild the French colonial empire in North America, the loss of Haiti, the richest colony in the Caribbean, significantly weakened France and undermined its colonial ambitions. Faced with growing economic difficulties and the threat of war with Great Britain, Napoleon made the bold decision to sell Louisiana to Thomas Jefferson for $15 million, a transaction that nearly doubled the size of the United States and paved the way for unprecedented westward expansion, leaving an indelible mark on history. At the same time, a wave of Haitian exiles, including French settlers, freedmen, and slaves, found refuge in New Orleans, bringing with them a cultural richness that transformed the city into a melting pot of diversity. Haiti's heroic struggle inspired other oppressed communities, igniting the flame of revolt and hope for equality and civil rights.

"The impact of Haiti's independence extended far beyond its redrawn borders", Telfort says proudly. The efforts of our brave leaders sought to export this revolution throughout the region, reaching out to revolutionaries in South America in their struggle to free themselves from the yoke of slavery and colonialism. Like a pilgrim of freedom, Haiti set itself up as a bastion of emancipation, determined to light the way to liberation for oppressed peoples. In doing so, it became the shining beacon of human emancipation throughout the world. This period represented a profound redefinition of cultural identities and an interweaving of peoples' struggles. Haiti's legacy continues to influence our world today, reminding us all that the quest for dignity and justice transcends age, borders, and race. In every cry of rebellion, in every step toward emancipation, the living echo of this great epic resounds, a hymn of resistance and hope whose torches still light the way for those who aspire to freedom.

The revolution of freedom that Haiti led for the benefit of humanity opened a path to universal emancipation that few nations have dared to take. But despite these epic achievements, Haiti often remains the most unloved of nations. Its sons and daughters, forced into exile, are displaced by migration policies that obscure the historical weight and cultural richness of their homeland. In their quest for recognition, they carry with them the legacy of a people who defied injustice, while facing the indifference of a world that, without the slightest conscience, chooses to ignore Haiti's vibrant light.

The United States, France, Spain, the Dominican Republic, and so many other nations owe the Republic of Haiti a debt of blood, yet they are often the first to deny its greatness. Are they afraid to see this small country regain its former glory and reassert itself as a leader on the chessboard of world powers? Alexandre Telfort's cry still echoes in our hearts, reminding us of all that the truth of our history cannot be suppressed. It embodies not only the desire for a better future for our country but also the determination of every Haitian, wherever he or she may be, to claim their right to dignity, justice, and prosperity. Haiti's rebirth is inevitable because the strength of its people is rooted in the depths of their souls, always ready to rise up against unjust oblivion.

Telfort's words remind us that each generation has the responsibility to change the course of history. His call to action is a powerful reminder that our struggle cannot be limited to speeches or lamentations but must be translated into concrete actions aimed at building a Haiti where every voice is heard, and every dream is valued.

This call for another Haiti is not just a wish, it's a promise. A promise to never abandon our homeland, despite the distance, to work tirelessly for a future of peace, justice, and equality. It urges us to come together, to join forces, to build bridges between our diaspora experiences and our Haitian roots, and to work together toward the realization of our collective vision.

By incorporating this rallying cry into our history, we choose hope. We pledge to be agents of change, to transform challenges into opportunities, and to celebrate the richness of our culture and resilience. This collective cry of awakened conscience for another Haiti is our most precious legacy, and it's up to us to make it resonate around the world to inspire not only our community but future generations.

As you turn these pages, you'll discover stories of immigrants who, like the author, are determined to overcome the challenges of their journey. They embody the resilience, strength, and creativity of a people who refuse to let circumstance define their future. Their stories are a source of inspiration and a powerful reminder that despite hardship, human dignity and the desire for freedom remain unshakable.

May each reader find a part of their own or their ancestors' story in this book, inviting them to understand the need to rethink immigration not only from a political perspective but from a shared human conscience.

I invite you to embark on this journey into the heart of awakened consciousness. A journey where the immigrant experience becomes a universal lesson in humanity, resilience and hope.

Jean Ronald Legouté, M.A.
Political scientist and economic development expert Speechwriter
for public authorities

PRELIMINARY NOTE

The Haitian community in Springfield, Ohio, has recently been confronted with incendiary rhetoric, including false and racist claims propagated by JD Vance and Donald Trump during their political campaigns. They have spread unfounded rumors that Haitian migrants are responsible for extreme acts such as kidnapping and eating pets, including cats and dogs. These allegations, which have no factual basis, caused major unrest in the city, leading to bomb threats and school closures. These allegations have spread around the world until they prompted the Dominican government to launch a massive expulsion of Haitians, with all the discrimination and racism that this entails.

This anti-immigrant rhetoric, supported by extremist groups such as the Blood Tribe, has exacerbated the polarization and stigmatization of migrants in the region. Local leaders such as Springfield Mayor Rob Rue and Ohio Governor Mike DeWine have strongly denounced these lies and called for peace and solidarity within the community. They pointed out that the majority of Haitian migrants in Springfield are here legally under protection programs.

These statements have serious implications for community relations and the safety of Haitian families, who have become targets of increased threats and violence. Misinformation, particularly on social networks, has amplified these tensions, reinforcing the idea that such rhetoric not only has a political impact but also endangers the lives and well-being of communities.

FOREWORD

A Journey to the Heart of My Conscience

Immigration is a universal experience, a path taken by millions of people across ages and continents. While others walked thousands of miles voluntarily, our grandparents were forced to cross oceans. But for each person, the journey is unique, shaped by personal stories, struggles, and hopes. Any of us can live this experience and not know it, and not have an immigrant conscience. The book you are about to read, Consciences of an Immigrant, is an intimate and reflective look at life as an immigrant in the United States. Through this story, we venture into the heart of the migratory experience and the issues at stake today, exploring the complex realities of being an immigrant in a country often perceived as the Promised Land. The America which has always been the land of immigrants is definitely expressing itself differently in the 2024 elections; and it's speaking out loudly against Haitian immigrants in Springfield, Ohio. There's an America that seems content to inflict more pain on those who have fled pain? The torment of discrimination that American leaders export as far away as the Dominican Republic is as if we've lost the right to be at peace wherever we are on earth.

Why this book?

It would be remiss of me, as a Haitian, if I didn't speak out at this time about the fate of our brothers and sisters, our common fate as discriminated immigrants. Because, in my humble opinion, the descendants of immigrants and the new immigrants need to talk to each other; because the new immigrants, wherever they come from, need to talk to each other; because the old diaspora and the new diaspora need to talk to each other. This is not a book about a particular situation, it's an ongoing dialogue. So, we wanted the immigrant reader to find through the lines an understanding of his or her reality and ways to integrate, while the reader who is a descendant of an immigrant takes a trip back in time to the history of his or her parents and grandparents. But the fundamental question underlying this book is why an immigrant, in this case a Haitian, feels the need to share his understanding today. To understand this need, it is crucial to examine the personal and collective context of Haitian immigration to the United States, a context rich in challenges, resilience, and hope.

The journey of a Haitian immigrant is often marked by experiences that are both deeply personal and universal. For many, leaving Haiti is the result of a desperate search for better living conditions, far from the hardships that shaped their existence in their homeland. It hasn't always been this way if we analyze the different waves of immigrants we've had over the years. But endemic poverty, devastating natural disasters, political crises, and daily struggles are all factors that drive people to seek a better future elsewhere. But the road to the promised land is far from straightforward. It is fraught with pitfalls and challenges that go far beyond the romantic notion of a new beginning.

The Haitian Experience: Background and Reflection

Haiti, a country with immense human and cultural resources, is often portrayed in a gloomy light because of its many socio-economic and political challenges. Behind this facade, however, lies a story of resilience and vibrant culture. Haitians who leave their homeland do so not only to escape misery, but also to give their children opportunities they never had, to seek stability, and to contribute to a better world.

Haitian immigration to the United States is not just a question of geographic displacement; it's also a question of identity, culture, and survival. Haitians bring with them a unique cultural richness that often mixes with American culture in complex ways. The contrast between expectations of a better life and the reality of integration into a new country raises profound questions about identity, belonging, and dignity.

The challenges and realities of immigration

The Haitian immigrant's journey is fraught with challenges that go far beyond the practical aspects of relocation. Upon arrival in the United States, an immigrant is confronted with a multitude of new realities: language, weather, legal system, social norms, and cultural values may be radically different from what he or she is accustomed to. This confrontation with a new environment can lead to profound culture shock, but also to opportunities for personal and collective enrichment.

The reality of immigration is often characterized by a double challenge: the need to reinvent oneself in a new environment, and the difficulty of maintaining and preserving one's cultural roots and identity. For Haitians, this can mean a constant effort to balance the expectations of the host society while preserving the traditions and values inherited from their country of origin.

An Intimate Look at Identity and Culture

Through the pages of this book, you'll discover not only the challenges faced by Haitian immigrants but also their significant contributions to American society. One of the goals of this book is to give voice to the Haitians who, despite the obstacles, have managed to create dynamic, thriving communities. Their presence enriches the cultural mosaic of the United States and brings a unique and valuable perspective to American culture.

The experiences described in this book are also a testament to the resilience and determination of Haitian immigrants. By telling these stories, we hope to provide a more nuanced and profound understanding of what it means to be a Haitian immigrant in the United States. These personal accounts remind us that immigration is a universal human experience, marked by hopes and challenges, but also by the ability to reinvent oneself and thrive in new circumstances.

The Ultimate Goal: Awakening Consciences

"*Consciences of an Immigrant*" aims to raise awareness of the realities experienced by Haitian immigrants and, more broadly, of the immigrant experience in general. By exploring the challenges, successes, and struggles of Haitian immigrants, this book seeks to foster a more open and empathetic dialogue on immigration issues.

We live in a time when immigration issues are often polarized and the subject of acrimonious debate. This book aims to contribute to a more enlightened and humane discussion by highlighting the perspectives and voices of people who live these realities on a daily basis. By sharing these experiences, we hope not only to inform but also to inspire action that promotes the integration and inclusion of immigrants.

A call to reflection and action

In conclusion, "*Consciences of an Immigrant*" is not only the sharing of certain personal consciences, but also a call for deeper reflection on the nature of immigration, identity, and integration. It invites us to rethink our perceptions of immigration and to recognize the valuable contribution that immigrants make to our societies.

The story of Haitian immigrants is one of courage, resilience, and transformation. It's a story that deserves to be heard, understood, and celebrated.

Through this book, we hope to offer an enriching perspective on the Haitian immigrant experience while contributing to a broader conversation about how we can build a more just, inclusive, and empathetic society for all. We also invite all communities to better organize themselves, especially the Haitian community, to move forward in a society in transition.

We invite you to read these pages with an open mind and heightened sensitivity, recognizing that each story is a reflection of the universal human experience. The challenges we face as immigrants, the successes we celebrate, and the hopes we nurture are the same as those shared by millions of people around the world. By listening and better understanding one another, we can build stronger bridges and create a brighter future for all.

INTRODUCTION

Michel de Montaigne, the famous French Renaissance philosopher, has been expressing profound reflections on human nature and travel since the 16th century in his *Essais*. When he says, "It is not the man who makes the journey, but the journey that makes the man," he is suggesting that the experience of travel transforms the person more than the individual controls the effects of that experience.

For Montaigne, travel is not just a physical displacement, but an opportunity to encounter new ideas, cultures, and ways of thinking that shape and enrich the human being. By exposing man to the diversity of the world and to self-discovery, travel becomes a process of inner formation, an intellectual and spiritual journey. It is this transformation, often unforeseen, that forges the traveler's character and understanding. For example, Montaigne observed from his own travels in Europe that one always returns differently, with a broader perspective on life and oneself. In his view, travel is a means of education, a mirror through which one can learn more about oneself and reinvent oneself.

I like to think of migration as a journey, first of all a journey into the unknown, a search for new horizons, but above all it's about meeting others. Leaving one's country of origin means embarking on an adventure in which one is confronted with different cultures, new traditions, and different perspectives. It's a process marked by the acceptance of change, by the discovery of another place that gradually becomes a new home.

Meeting others through immigration means opening oneself to difficult dialogues, to different ways of life, but also to moments of sharing and mutual enrichment. Each immigrant brings a part of his or her culture, history, and identity, which he or she confronts with that of the host country. It's a meeting of dreams, hopes, and sometimes harsh realities, but this interaction creates a rich exchange, a complex web of reciprocal influences.

Immigration, although often perceived as uprooting people, is actually an opportunity to build bridges between people. It's a way to break down the barriers of fear, misunderstanding, and prejudice, to learn to live together, to respect and complement each other. In meeting others, we redefine our common humanity.

Beyond the challenges of immigration, it reminds us that the world is a vast terrain of encounters, where each step toward the other is an invitation to better understand, to better unite, and to build together a more inclusive and united future.

It's often surprising to realize that immigration is not a one-way phenomenon, with the U.S. being a land of welcome only for foreigners. In fact, some 7.5 million Americans have chosen to live abroad, becoming "expatriates" in various countries around the world. This figure highlights a little-discussed aspect of international mobility: that of Americans who, for a variety of reasons, choose to leave their home country. It's also surprising that they are identified as "expatriates" and not as migrants like everyone else; they come from wealthy countries and more. It's a fact that a Haitian expert who immigrates to the United States for professional reasons remains a migrant; a Caucasian American expert who immigrates to Haiti, on the other hand, is an expatriate. An American expert of Haitian origin who immigrates to Haiti for professional reasons is not an expatriate.

In any case, the motivations behind this migration are as varied as the individual journeys. Some leave for professional opportunities, to broaden their horizons in a dynamic economic environment, or to escape a country that is not for them or that has taken everything from them. Others are motivated by personal reasons: joining a foreign spouse, exploring a new culture, or simply living an adventure. And then there are those who, lured by a more affordable cost of living or a more accessible health care system, choose to spend their retirement in more favorable destinations.

This phenomenon of American migration abroad reflects a global reality: the world is increasingly interconnected, and mobility is becoming an accessible option for many citizens, even those from countries considered economically stable and prosperous. There are Americans who can't make it in the U.S., who are forced to seek life elsewhere, not on the moon, but among other people.

However, living abroad is not always without its challenges. Adapting to a new language, different customs, or foreign bureaucratic systems can be difficult, and these expatriates often face the same challenges as immigrants to the U.S. They must find a balance between integrating into their host country and maintaining their American identity.

Ultimately, the reality of the 7.5 million Americans living abroad demonstrates that immigration and emigration are reciprocal phenomena, enriching both host societies and countries of origin. It reminds us that migration is a universal human experience, characterized by openness to others, the search for new opportunities, and the ability to adapt to increasingly diverse environments.

Why this book? Why did I, as an immigrant, feel the need to take up the pen and put down my thoughts and reflections? The answer is complex and, in many ways, deeply personal. This book is not only an expression of my experience as an immigrant in the United States, but also a way for the man of character that I am to speak out for our people, and to always stand up for dignity and justice. I made a statement about the attacks against us, which I'm honored to share with you in the appendix, but my heart told me it wasn't enough. I had to give more, to try to make visible voices that are too often ignored, to demystify the migratory experience, and to question a system that, although rooted in the principles of freedom and equality, sometimes seems to forget these fundamental values when it comes to welcoming those who seek refuge, opportunity or simply a better future.

Migration without an immigration plan

My story is not unique or exceptional. It's the story of millions of people around the world. It begins long before I arrived on American soil, long before I was confronted with the administrative maze of immigration, long before I understood what it really means to be a "foreigner" in a country that prides itself on being a nation of immigrants.

I arrived in Trump's America with no intention of immigrating. My arrival was just a pit stop, a temporary stop. I had come from Italy, where I had landed after making the decision to bring my wife and children to the United States for safety reasons. It was all supposed to be temporary, a provisional situation until conditions in Haiti stabilized.

I was at the height of my career at the time. I was working as an advisor to the President of the Republic of Haiti, a prestigious position that allowed me to influence the political decisions of the country. At the same time, I was president of a political party, a responsibility that opened the door to the next elections. My wife, on the other hand, held an important position in an American NGO. Our children attended the best schools in Port-au-Prince. We led a life that, despite the turbulence of the country, had a certain balance, a certain order. I was president of the newly formed Ayiti2054 party, hundreds of young people looked to me for leadership, and the idea of staying in the United States to rebuild our lives never crossed our minds.

23

But the COVID-19 pandemic changed everything. It upended our plans and forced us to extend our stay here. What was supposed to be a temporary visit turned into an indefinite stay. With each passing day, the situation in Haiti worsened. Violence increased, security disintegrated, and finally, on July 7, 2021, President Jovenel Moïse was assassinated in his home, an event that marked a definitive turning point in our thinking about the future.

Meanwhile, back in the States, I was in for another shock. The death of George Floyd, who suffocated under a policeman's knee, sparked a wave of anger and demonstrations across the country. The black American community, to which I felt a natural connection, was rising up against a profound and systemic injustice. It was an emotional moment, a historic moment, but paradoxically it made America less welcoming to those of us who were only thinking of going home.

Here we were, in a country we loved to visit for short trips, Christmas vacations, or summer getaways, but where the idea of staying, of rebuilding our lives, seemed unthinkable. I remember turning down several offers of diplomatic posts before the president's death, convinced that my future and that of my family lay in Haiti, not elsewhere.

But something unexpected was happening before our eyes. Our children, who had initially struggled to assimilate, were becoming more integrated. They were beginning to speak English fluently and, even more surprisingly, they seemed happy. Their adjustment to this new country was much faster than ours. Their smiles and fluency in this new language gave me pause. We usually kept them at home, worried about their health and safety. We were reluctant to take them to the parks or the movies, but they were thriving.

This caused me to do some soul-searching. I realized that while we adults still felt a deep connection to Haiti, our children were building their own reality here. They were adopting this culture, immersing themselves in this society, and that forced us to rethink our future. Were we going to rip them away from this burgeoning happiness and take them back to an increasingly unstable Haiti? Could we still turn back the clock while they were already on their way here without even realizing it?

Every day that passed added to my inner dilemma. My role as a father, and a protector, drove me to give them the best life possible, but my attachment to my homeland tormented me. How could I leave my country, my political responsibilities, my plans for the future, all those comrades who carried the flame of change within them? How could I imagine building something here when my whole heart, my whole identity was rooted in Haiti? And the melancholy begins to weaken you, and when you miss Haiti, it's an inexplicable suffering.

Immigration is much more than a simple geographical change. It's an intimate journey, a complete revision of our certainties, our choices, and our values. And that journey, the one that brought me to Trump's America, changed me.

I was born in a country where travel is considered a privilege reserved for the fortunate few, a luxury to which the majority have no access. So true, in fact, that you're not supposed to talk about leaving because it could get you killed. They'll kill you because you'll become an immigrant. In this part of the world, going abroad, especially to the world's leading power, is a rare, almost mythical opportunity. It's like a sesame seed to another reality, a promise of a better future, or at least a break from the harshness of daily life. I belong to a generation that saw being born on American soil as an extraordinary gift, a privilege that destiny reserved for a chosen few. To have a child in the United States was to guarantee that child a life of opportunity, a chance, access to rights, and prospects that many would never experience.

But my wife and I didn't give in. We didn't go with the flow. We believed deeply that our place was in our own country and that our children's destiny should not be determined by a birth number or a visa. We believed in our ability to give them a full life, even in the difficult conditions of our country. We were among those who still believed that the future was built where we had planted our roots, and that exile, however tempting, was not always the best solution.

I'm also part of a generation that has often seen some of its peers leave school to chase the dream of permanent residence in a foreign country. Over the years, I've seen friends and family put their education on hold in hopes of obtaining that precious document, the famous "green card," that would open the doors to a different life. For many, it was a long and sometimes fruitless quest, but it was seen as the only way to a measure of security, a hope for prosperity.

And yet, through it all, there's one thing that has remained steadfast about us as a nation: our hospitality. The immigrant, whether from near or far, is king with us. It's a tradition, almost an unwritten rule, to welcome others with kindness, to offer them shelter, a meal, and a sympathetic ear. We don't question the origin of those who knock on our door. We welcome them. It's a value we cherish because deep down we know what it means to be uprooted, to be lost, to seek refuge. We know what it means to leave everything behind, to seek elsewhere what can no longer be found at home. In our veins is the love of those who leave their homeland to come to us. Our ancestors passed on this legacy to us, which is why we like to call Haiti the land of freedom.

This hospitality, this generosity to strangers, is at the heart of our identity. It reminds us that despite the difficulties, the poverty, and the crises that shake our country, we remain committed to the human person. We know what it means to be vulnerable, and that's why we open our doors. For us, immigration is not just a political or economic act. It's a bond of humanity. It's the recognition that behind every exile there is a story, a person, a family, and dreams.

We are a people who, although often forced to flee, never forget where we come from. And in this collective memory there is always a place for the other. It is this culture, this spirit of welcome, that keeps us deeply rooted in our values even in foreign lands. And that may be our greatest strength.

The need to give voice

Over the years, I've come to realize that my story, while deeply personal, has been shared by many others. I've seen men and women from all walks of life face the same challenges, the same fears, the same uncertainties. I saw people sacrificing everything they had to give their children a better future, and yet they were viewed with suspicion, even contempt.

It was this reality, this gap between dream and reality, between perception and truth, that led me to write this book. We live in a time when immigration is at the center of passionate, polarizing debates when political discourse tends to reduce people to numbers, statistics, and problems to be solved. It's easy, too easy, to dehumanize others when you don't know their stories when you can only see the surface of things.

In writing this book, I want to show that behind every immigrant there is a story, a life, dreams, and aspirations. That behind every decision to leave, there are often complex reasons, political, economic and social contexts that push people to leave their country, sometimes at the risk of their lives. I want this book to be a bridge, a way to understand others, to look beyond stereotypes and prejudices.

A changing American context

Are we too late in an America that's too old? The immigration debate in the United States is particularly complex and emotionally charged. This country, built on successive waves of immigrants, now seems to be wavering on how to approach the issue. On the one hand, there's the glorious narrative of America as a land of welcome, a beacon for those seeking freedom and a chance to succeed. On the other, there's a growing fear of the outsider, a suspicion fueled by divisive political rhetoric and an identity crisis about what it means to be

American. Do new immigrants seem to offer a mirror to remind an America that wants to forget where it came from?

As an immigrant, I've experienced these contradictions firsthand. On the one hand, we're told we're welcome, that we're needed for the economy, for cultural diversity, for innovation. On the other hand, we are confronted with increasingly restrictive policies, with rhetoric that portrays us as a threat, as intruders.

This book was born out of that frustration, that feeling of being caught between two contradictory narratives. I want to show that immigration is not a problem to be solved, but a reality to be understood, a richness to be embraced. Yes, there are challenges, and legitimate questions about how to integrate newcomers, about the economic and social impact. But these challenges shouldn't make us lose sight of the essential: immigration is above all a human story.

From the individual to the collective

In writing *Consciences of an Immigrant*, I also hope to strike a deeper, more universal chord. Beyond my own experience, I want to question our common humanity. What drives us to reject others, to build walls, real or symbolic, between us? Why is it so difficult to welcome others, to see them not as a threat, but as a potential, source of mutual enrichment?

Through my encounters, experiences, and reflections, I hope to show that we all have something to gain from opening our minds and hearts. The real danger to society is not the arrival of newcomers, but turning inward, fearing the other, forgetting our core values. American history, like that of so many other nations, is punctuated by moments when we have risen above our fears, embraced change, and grown from it.

A call to conscience

This book is a call to that collective consciousness, to the ability we all have to see beyond appearances, to recognize the humanity of others. As an immigrant, I didn't just leave a country. I left a life, a story, a part of myself. And like so many others, I'm trying to rebuild, to reinvent myself, to contribute in my own way to this new country that has welcomed me, sometimes reluctantly, sometimes generously.

But this book is also a call to my immigrant brothers and sisters. We have a role to play, a responsibility. We have a responsibility not to let prejudice and hate speech define us, but to show through our actions, our work, and our commitment, that we are a positive force, a driving force for change. We must tell our stories and share our experiences so that our children and our children's children can live in a more just and inclusive world.

In short, *Consciences of an Immigrant* is a work that aims to raise awareness of the plight of migrants and to rehumanize debates about immigration. Offering both an intimate and universal perspective, the book poses essential questions: How can we live up to the values we profess? How can we give everyone the chance to live in dignity, no matter where they come from? Whatever the color of their skin.

It's time to change the narrative, to take control of our own story. It's time to say loud and clear that we are more than numbers, more than residence permits, more than foreigners. We are human beings with dreams, hopes, and talents. We are full members of this society, and our voices deserve to be heard.

This book is my contribution to this change. It's a gesture of resistance in the face of indifference, an act of faith in the future, a declaration of love for this country that, despite its contradictions and imperfections, has given me a chance. A chance to live, to grow, to contribute. A chance to dream and to write. The immigration debate is more than a question of borders or quotas; it's a question of human conscience.

The challenges of migration

Behind every immigrant is a unique story, but also a journey fraught with pitfalls. For many of us, arriving in the United States, while eagerly anticipated, is often synonymous with disillusionment. We arrive with our heads full of dreams, convinced that our skills, qualifications, and determination to succeed will be enough to overcome any obstacles. But from the very first steps, we are faced with seemingly insurmountable challenges: the language barrier, the culture shock, the lack of social and professional networks, not to mention the administrative and legal difficulties involved in obtaining a stable legal status.

Far from reinforcing stereotypes of the "lazy" or "profiteering" immigrant, these difficulties demonstrate our resilience and courage. It takes incredible strength to leave everything behind and reinvent oneself in an environment where every gesture, every word is subject to the gaze of others. We must learn quickly, adapt constantly, juggle multiple identities, and cope with intense psychological pressure.

Integration: a shared challenge

Integration is not a one-way street. It's not only up to the immigrant to adapt to the host society; it's also up to the host society to recognize the value and potential contributions of those it receives. We all know that when we come here, we want to participate in and contribute to the greatness of a country that offers humanity. Yet the current debate on immigration tends to portray integration as a burden, a liability, and even a threat to national cohesion. Too often we forget that, far from dividing people, immigration can strengthen the social fabric, stimulate innovation, and enrich culture.

This book seeks to highlight the stories of those who, like me, have struggled to integrate, not by denying their origins, but by bringing a part of themselves to their new home. I'm thinking of the Syrian doctor who fought against prejudice to have his qualifications recognized and who now saves lives in a Midwestern hospital. I'm thinking of the young Guatemalan student who came here illegally and, through her hard work, won a scholarship to a prestigious university. I'm thinking of the Haitian, Nigerian, and Pakistani entrepreneurs who are creating jobs and stimulating local economies.

These stories are not anomalies. They reflect the best of what immigration brings: energy, creativity, and a deep commitment to success. But for these successes to multiply, for these inspiring stories to become the norm, we need to change our perspective, to see immigration not as a threat, but as an opportunity.

The misperception of immigrants

In the collective imagination, immigrants are often perceived through the narrow prism of threat: they take our jobs, burden our welfare system, and threaten our security. These perceptions, fueled by populist rhetoric and sensationalist media, obscure a very different reality.

The majority of immigrants don't come here to "steal" anything. They come to contribute, to participate, to build. They often take jobs that locals don't want, work in difficult conditions, and invest in their children's education so that they, in turn, can realize their dreams. The immigrant is much more than "Cheap Labor"; they are people with skills, talents, and aspirations. When given the opportunity, they can become key players in the economic, social, and cultural development of the country.

The economic contribution of immigrants

It's important to remember that immigrants play a critical role in the American economy. According to several studies, immigrants contribute more in taxes than they receive in social services. They start businesses at a higher rate than natives, spur innovation, especially in technology, and fill gaps in the labor market; labor shortages in key sectors such as agriculture, healthcare, and construction.

But beyond the numbers, there's another, more intangible dimension to immigrants' contributions. They bring fresh perspectives, different ways of thinking, and cultures that enrich the social fabric. They build bridges between the United States and the rest of the world, facilitating cultural, commercial, and diplomatic exchanges.

At its best, America has always valued this diversity. Successive waves of immigration - whether Irish, Italian, Chinese, or, more recently, Latino and African - have at one time or another provoked fear and resistance. But over time, these communities have integrated, helping to shape the American identity and demonstrating that diversity is not an obstacle but an asset.

The urgent need for reform

The U.S. immigration system as it exists today is not only inefficient, but also unfair. It leaves millions of people in limbo, creates unacceptable humanitarian situations, and deprives the country of valuable talent and skills. We urgently need to reform this system to make it more humane, more flexible, and better suited to the realities of the 21st century.

But to do that, we need to change the way we look at immigration. We must understand that behind every visa denied, behind every family separated, behind every asylum claim denied, there are lives shattered, and hopes dashed. We must understand that immigration is not an abstract question of laws and borders, but a profoundly human issue. We must have the courage to listen to these stories, to open our hearts and minds, to see the other not as an intruder, but as a brother or sister.

Hope for the future

I deeply believe that the United States has the potential to once again become that land of welcome, that beacon of freedom and opportunity. But it won't happen without a conscious effort on the part of everyone: politicians, citizens, immigrants. We must all join the conversation, reject the rhetoric of hate and division, and work together to build a society that is more just, more inclusive, and more true to its ideals.

This book is my contribution to that effort. It is an attempt to reconcile the American dream with the reality of immigrants. It's a call to conscience, a reminder that we all have the right as human beings to seek a better life, to realize our dreams, to live in dignity.

I believe that words have the power to change hearts, to change minds, to inspire empathy. Because I believe that the story of immigration is the story of humanity. Because at the end of the day, what we're all looking for, whether we were born here or somewhere else, is the same thing: a better life for ourselves and our children, a chance to contribute, to create, to leave a mark, our little place in the sun.

In writing this book, I want to say to immigrants: you are not alone. Your struggles, your hopes, your dreams are shared by millions of others. To those who doubt the contributions of immigrants, I say: open your hearts and minds, listen to our stories.

You'll see that we are not the cause of your misfortune.

CHAPTER ONE

CONSCIENCE OF WHERE WE COME FROM

The path for Haitian immigrants to the United States was paved with the blood, sweat and sacrifice of our ancestors; with honor and bravery in one of the bloodiest battles of the American Revolution; the Battle of Savannah in Georgia between September and October 1779. It's a path marked by the vision and hard work of a man from Saint-Marc who crossed America to found one of the greatest and most beautiful cities in the United States. And also, by the dignity of workers of all kinds, creators, inventors, designers, and so on. We need to share with you where we come from, to understand from the Haitian example that this is not a natural fate destined for immigrants, but a deliberate choice to prevent us from living because we're the descendants of the first black people.

Let's take a look at two, or three most important facts of history:

The Battle of Savannah

The year was 1779 and the American Revolution was in full swing. The thirteen British colonies were trying to throw off the yoke of the British Empire, and one of the decisive battles was fought in Savannah, Georgia. Against this backdrop, some 800 black men from Saint-Domingue (now Haiti) distinguished themselves by their bravery and devotion to the American cause.

These soldiers were part of the French army allied with the Americans in their fight against the British. They belonged to the "chasseurs-volontaires de Saint-Domingue" regiment, a unit composed primarily of black soldiers and free men of color. At the time, Haiti, then a French colony, was a slave society, but a minority of free blacks had managed to gain some status. Many of them, while aware of the contradictions of their situation, had a deep desire for freedom and equality that led them to join the War of Independence as allies of France.

On October 9, 1779, during the siege of Savannah, these 800 Haitians fought alongside American and French troops against the British army. This battle was one of the bloodiest of the American Revolution, and although the allies failed to retake Savannah, the courage of the Haitian soldiers left a lasting impression. Coming from a colony where slavery was still rampant, these men fought for the freedom of another people, perhaps hoping that one day the same freedom would be granted to them.

One of the most famous of these volunteers was Henri Christophe, who would later become one of the leaders of the Haitian Revolution and the first post-independence king of Haiti. The participation of these soldiers in the American War of Independence left a lasting mark not only on the history of the United States, but also on that of Haiti, as it fostered the spirit of revolt that would lead to the Haitian Revolution.

The story of the Battle of Savannah shows that American independence was not won by European settlers alone, but also thanks to the contributions of men and women from diverse backgrounds, including the French colonies. These Haitian soldiers brought not only their physical strength to the battlefield but also their moral support, embodying solidarity in the universal quest for freedom.

Yet this contribution has long been overlooked, and erased from history, yet their commitment symbolizes the interconnectedness of independence struggles around the world. By helping the United States gain its independence, these Haitians laid the groundwork for their own struggle for freedom, a struggle that would erupt a few years later with the Haitian Revolution of 1791.

The founding of the city of Chicago

The story of the founding of the city of Chicago is marked by an often overlooked but essential figure: Jean Baptiste Pointe du Sable, a Haitian who played a central role in the creation of what would become one of the greatest cities in the United States. Born in Haiti in the mid-1800s, du Sable is recognized as Chicago's first non-native permanent resident and is often referred to as the "Father of Chicago".

Jean Baptiste Pointe du Sable was born in the French colony of Saint-Domingue (now Haiti), probably around 1745. His father was French and his mother an African slave. At the time, Haitian society was marked by strong racial tensions and divisions between white settlers, free people of color, and slaves. As a free mulatto, du Sable undoubtedly sought to distance himself from the conflicts of his homeland in order to forge a future in the New World.

Accounts of his arrival in North America vary, but it appears that he left Haiti in his youth, first for French Louisiana and then for the British colonies farther north. His journey took him to the Great Lakes region, where he met and married a woman of Potawatomi descent, Catherine, with whom he had two children. This alliance with the Potawatomi allowed him to integrate and skillfully navigate the complex relationship between European settlers and Native Americans.

In the 1770s, Jean Baptiste Pointe du Sable settled at the mouth of the Chicago River, a strategic location on the shores of Lake Michigan. At the time, the region was sparsely populated, inhabited primarily by Native American tribes. Du Sable built a large wooden house and established a trading post that quickly became a thriving center of commerce. He bartered with the Indians and traded furs, grain, and other goods with European settlers and voyageurs.

His establishment, simple at first, grew rapidly. He added stables, a blacksmith shop, a bakery, a dairy, an orchard, and even a ballroom. His trading post became the economic heart of the region, attracting not only merchants but also adventurers, travelers, and soldiers. In just a few years, du Sable transformed what had been a swamp into a vibrant center of activity, laying the groundwork for what would become the city of Chicago.

Its prosperity and influence were also enhanced by its integration into local communities. Despite the racial prejudices of the time, Jean Baptiste Pointe du Sable was respected by both Native Americans and European settlers. His mastery of several languages, including French, English, and Amerindian dialects, enabled him to navigate skillfully between these different cultures. This ability to act as a bridge between peoples and cultures made him a key figure in the region.

Despite his success, du Sable remained a retiring man, and his reasons for leaving Chicago in the 1800s remain a mystery. In 1800, he sold his business to another pioneer, John Kinzie, and left the region to settle near St. Charles, Missouri, where he died in 1818.

Today, the legacy of Jean Baptiste Pointe Du Sable is widely recognized in Chicago. In 1968, a bridge over the Chicago River was named in his honor, and in 2006, a central city square was renamed Pioneer Court, where a statue of Pointe du Sable stands. In addition, the DuSable Museum of African American

History in Chicago bears his name and commemorates his contributions to the city's history and African American heritage.

Jean Baptiste Pointe du Sable is a symbol of Haitian and African American influence in the building of the United States. His story embodies that of many black immigrants who, despite obstacles, managed to integrate into society and contribute significantly to the building of new communities. Though his role was long ignored, he is now celebrated as a pioneer whose vision and work laid the foundation for one of America's most iconic cities.

Ultimately, Jean Baptiste Pointe du Sable was much more than a merchant; he was the founder of a city that would become a global cultural and economic crossroads. His contribution demonstrates that the history of the United States is a mosaic of diverse narratives, in which immigrants and people of color have played a fundamental role. Today, Chicago stands proudly as a living monument to its heritage, reminding us that individuals like du Sable, from often unexpected backgrounds, have shaped the history of an entire nation.

Founding the « New World »

In 1804, Haiti founded a new world, not only by declaring its independence, but also by making a revolutionary act unprecedented in human history. It was the first free black republic in the modern world, and the first country to overthrow the slave system at the heart of the colonial empire. By breaking the chains of oppression, Haiti marked a historic turning point, laying the foundation for a new world in which equality and freedom would become not just ideals but realities for those who had been reduced to property.

The context of this Haitian revolution, part of the long struggle of oppressed peoples for human dignity, is essential to understanding Haiti's global impact on the world. Saint Domingue, then a French colony, was known as the "Pearl of the Antilles" because of its economic wealth, fueled by the forced labor of slaves on sugar, coffee, and indigo plantations. The colony was vital to France, accounting for a large portion of its colonial revenues. However this inhumane system was based on the suffering, oppression, and exploitation of a population of African slaves.

When the slaves of Saint-Domingue, inspired by the ideals of the French Revolution - liberty, equality, fraternity - revolted in 1791, they launched a war that would last more than a decade. Led by leaders such as Toussaint Louverture and Jean-Jacques Dessalines, they fought for independence with a determination that stunned the world. It was a struggle not only for individual freedom but for the recognition of human dignity and the abolition of the slave system that reduced people to commodities.

When Jean-Jacques Dessalines declared Haiti's independence on January 1, 1804, he not only created a new nation. He shook the foundations of the colonial and slave-owning world order. With its independence, Haiti became a beacon for the oppressed, not only in the Caribbean but throughout the world. Slaves on the plantations of the American South, colonized peoples in Africa, and even abolitionist movements in Europe found in Haiti a source of inspiration and hope. Haiti, this small Caribbean country, had shown that it was possible for the oppressed to throw off their chains and overthrow empires.

But beyond the symbolism of freedom, Haiti also laid the foundation for a new world by challenging the dominant racial and colonial structures. By overthrowing not only the slave system but also the colonial order, Haiti became a space in which new ideas about sovereignty, justice, and the equality of peoples could emerge. Dessalines' 1804 decree offering citizenship to any African or descendant of Africans willing to come and live in Haiti was a bold act of international solidarity, a call for the worldwide brotherhood of the oppressed.

This new symbolic order frightened the colonial powers. The United States, France, Britain, and other colonial nations, fearing that the Haitian example would provoke slave revolts in their own colonies, did everything in their power to isolate and marginalize Haiti. What followed was an international embargo, a policy of economic and diplomatic isolation designed to strangle the young republic. Yet despite this isolation, Haiti continued to play a crucial role in the formation of a new world.

Similarly, Haiti played a role in the affirmation of independence struggles throughout Latin America. Simon Bolivar, one of the great leaders of the liberation of South America, found refuge in Haiti in 1815 after being defeated by Spanish forces. In Haiti, he received support and assistance from Haitian President Alexandre Pétion. In return, Bolívar promised to free the slaves in the territories he would liberate in Latin America. This crucial support contributed to the success of the independence struggles on the South American continent and once again established Haiti as a key player in the creation of a new world.

Thus, in 1804, Haiti not only became the first free black republic in the modern world. It laid the foundation for a new order that recognized the dignity of all human beings, regardless of race or social background. Haiti's independence sent a shockwave that reverberated around the world and echoed in the struggles for freedom and justice that would follow for centuries to come.

The effects of this revolution are still being felt today, though they are often forgotten or ignored in traditional accounts of world history. But for those who seek to understand the roots of the struggle for human rights and equality, Haiti remains an indelible symbol of what it truly means to be free. In 1804, Haiti founded a new world - one in which freedom is not a privilege reserved for a few, but an inalienable right of every human being.

The Impact of Haitian Independence on Louisiana

Haiti's independence in 1804 had profound and unexpected consequences for Louisiana, playing a crucial role in the destiny of this region of the United States. The success of the revolution not only overturned the established order in the Caribbean, but also contributed to a significant shift in colonial power dynamics in North America. To understand the impact of Haitian independence on Louisiana, we must look back at French ambitions in the region. In 1800, Napoleon Bonaparte, then the First Consul of France, signed the Treaty of San Ildefonso, which ceded Louisiana to Spain. Napoleon planned to rebuild the French colonial empire in North America, and Louisiana was to play a central role in this project. However, the Haitian Revolution quickly changed his plans.

The loss of Haiti, the richest colony in the Caribbean, weakened France considerably. The economy of Saint-Domingue (now Haiti) was based on the intensive production of sugar, coffee, and other agricultural products that fed the French economy. With Haiti's independence, Napoleon not only lost this source of wealth but also realized that it would be extremely difficult to maintain his colonial ambitions in the New World without a solid economic base in the Caribbean.

This context played a major role in the sale of Louisiana to the United States in 1803. Faced with the threat of war with Great Britain and growing economic difficulties after the loss of Haiti, Napoleon decided to sell Louisiana to Thomas Jefferson for $15 million. This sale, known as the Louisiana Purchase, nearly doubled the size of the United States, giving it an immense territory and paving the way for its westward expansion with new states such as Arkansas, Oklahoma, Kansas, Missouri, Iowa, Nebraska, Colorado, South Dakota, Minnesota, Wyoming, North Dakota, and Montana.

But beyond this territorial and economic aspect, Haitian independence had social and cultural consequences for Louisiana. After the Haitian Revolution, a large number of French colonists, freedmen, and slaves fled from Saint-Domingue to New York and Louisiana, especially New Orleans. These refugees brought their culture, language, and social practices with them, increasing French and Creole influence in the region. The population of New Orleans became more diverse and cosmopolitan, with a significant presence of Haitian refugees who brought their music, cuisine, and a particular sense of resistance to oppression.

This wave of migration also had an impact on race relations in Louisiana. Haitian slaves and freedmen arriving in New Orleans fueled the desire for freedom among local slaves, exacerbating racial tensions in the region. Many white settlers feared that the example of the Haitian Revolution would inspire slave revolts in Louisiana and elsewhere in the American South. These fears influenced local policies on slave control and emancipation, leading to increased repression and the strengthening of black codes restricting the rights of freedmen.

In the end, Haitian independence and the sale of Louisiana to the United States were inextricably linked. The Haitian Revolution not only ended one of the most brutal colonial systems in history, but it also helped redraw the map of North America. Louisiana, once a centerpiece of the French imperial project, became a bastion of growth and expansion for the 13 American colonies. The passage of Haitian refugees into Louisiana enriched the region's Creole culture while accentuating social tensions over the issue of slavery. The Haitian Revolution shaped not only the history of Haiti but also the destiny of Louisiana, shaping both its territorial future and its cultural heritage.

Concern and fear underpin relations between Haiti and the United States

"Our policy toward Haiti has been set for years. We trade with that country, but we have no diplomatic relations. It doesn't send us mulatto consuls or black ambassadors... Why? Because keeping the peace of eleven of our states does not allow black ambassadors and consuls to come and show their black brethren that honors await them if they do as they do. We cannot permit them to come and say that it was the murder of their masters that earned them the friendship of the white people of the United States. U.S. Senator Thomas Hart Benton of Missouri made these striking remarks about U.S. policy toward Haiti, reflecting the mood of the times.

In 1824, he declared that under no circumstances should the United States recognize Haitian independence, which would pose a direct threat to the established social order, especially in the southern states where slavery was deeply entrenched. For Benton and his contemporaries, recognizing Haitian sovereignty was tantamount to legitimizing slave rebellion and encouraging insubordination on American plantations.

His statements were based on the fear that the Haitian Revolution would inspire similar uprisings among black slaves in the South. Haiti, after all, represented a victorious rebellion against one of the world's most powerful colonial powers: France. This slave-led revolution was an aberration in the minds of white American elites, who feared that the idea of freedom would cross borders and spread to the enslaved populations of the United States.

Benton saw Haiti as a destabilizing example, a nation that had defied the racial laws and social hierarchies on which so many American institutions were based. He therefore proposed a hard line: isolate Haiti, suppress any form of international recognition, and maintain a distance between this young black republic and other nations. This stance of continued non-recognition reflected a strategy of political containment aimed at preventing any challenge to the slave-owning order in the United States.

This policy of denying Haiti international recognition was not just Benton's opinion, but an official position that the United States maintained for decades, delaying diplomatic recognition of the world's first black republic until 1862. For Benton and many of his colleagues, the survival of the United States as they knew it depended on the marginalization of Haiti since the very existence of a free black nation posed a threat to white supremacy and the status quo. By refusing to recognize Haiti, the United States sought to maintain stable relations with France and preserve the international order dominated by the great colonial powers.

Benton's perspective underscores the link between U.S. foreign policy and the preservation of slavery within its own borders. Recognition of Haiti could have not only weakened the authority of slaveholders but also brought about a series of radical changes that would have challenged the very foundations of American society at the time.

Haitian independence has always been a source of concern for the United States, not only because of the revolution's direct impact on the colonial world order, but also because of the threat it posed to the American slave system. History shows us that Haitian independence, proclaimed in 1804 after a victorious slave revolt, overturned the established order, an order based on the exploitation of slaves and slavery, especially in the American South, where the economy depended heavily on slave labor.

Migration to the United States

After our independence in 1804 and throughout the 19th century until 1934, we in Haiti received more American immigrants than the United States received Haitians. The small nation had not yet finished celebrating its independence when the Father of the Nation gave us the guidelines for our brothers and sisters still under the yoke of slavery. On January 14, 1804, Jean-Jacques Dessalines promulgated a decree offering a reward of 40 piastres (the equivalent of 40 US dollars at the time) to any ship captain who agreed to repatriate enslaved Haitians and former slaves who had fled during the revolutionary conflicts. With this solemn act, Dessalines sought to recruit 500,000 Africans, indigenous peoples, and black Americans, offering them freedom and immediate citizenship upon their arrival on Haitian soil, provided they first declared themselves black. Many freedom lovers responded to this appeal.

After laying the groundwork, other Haitian presidents followed suit. About 13,000 under President Boyer in 1824, 12,000 under President Fabre Nicolas Geffrard, and not counting the 2,000 soldiers who occupied us and others in 1915. The United States was not the preferred destination, especially since it only recognized Haiti's independence in 1862. For the intellectuals, this was a trend that lasted until the 90s: the United States was a country for merchants, for those who didn't go to school, and for peasants who could do any kind of work. The first immigrants to New York, who settled in Harlem in particular, worked in the import, industrial, and commercial sectors, or in the liberal professions. They were the ones who drew the attention of black American intellectuals and journalists to what was happening in Haiti and mobilized them to defend Haiti against the American occupation.

Despite the American occupation of Haiti, the mass of immigrants preferred to seek work in Cuba, the Dominican Republic and the Bahamas, which we've known since 1790. For the intellectuals, literati and wealthy families, it was France and Belgium. By 1939, there were officially about 500 Haitians living in New York, and no Haitian colony was mentioned in Chicago.

With each wave of Haitian immigration to the United States, it seems inevitable that a major crisis will arise, often exacerbated by external factors, including political and economic intervention by the United States itself. The history of relations between Haiti and the United States is marked by episodes of successive crises that, in many cases, have served as catalysts for the mass exodus of Haitians to American shores. From the military occupation of 1915 to the intermittent support of unstable regimes, U.S. involvement in Haiti's internal affairs has directly or indirectly driven thousands of Haitians to seek refuge abroad, particularly in North America.

First wave of immigration: the 1915 American occupation

The first major wave of Haitian immigration to the United States dates back to the American occupation of Haiti from 1915 to 1934. Under the pretext of stabilizing a country torn apart by internal strife, the United States took control of Haiti and imposed military and economic domination. During this period, Haitian peasants were massively dispossessed of their land, and roads and infrastructure were built to serve mainly American interests. For many Haitians, this occupation was synonymous with dispossession, impoverishment and violent repression. Faced with growing instability and exacerbated inequalities, some of Haiti's elite, as well as desperate rural families, began to migrate to the United States, particularly to Florida, in search of a better life.

Second Wave: The Duvalier exile and the tacit complicity of the United States

In the 1960s and 1970s, Haiti was plunged into the Duvalier dictatorship, a dark period marked by decades of political repression, state violence, and terror organized by the militias known as the Tonton Macoutes. This regime thrived in part because of economic and political support from the United States, which turned a blind eye to human rights abuses in Haiti under the guise of fighting communism. Many Haitians fled this brutal regime, often with the tacit approval or indifference of American authorities who feared an unstable Haiti falling under Soviet influence.

America welcomed the elite fleeing François Duvalier's repression while remaining discreet about the military and logistical support provided to his regime. During this period, thousands of Haitian refugees began to settle in cities such as New York and Miami, creating a large and influential diaspora.

Third wave: the end of the dictatorship and post-Duvalier instability

After the overthrow of Jean-Claude Duvalier in 1986, Haiti entered a long period of political transition marked by chronic instability. American intervention in this period of "democratic transition" was ambiguous, especially with the 1991 coup that overthrew Jean-Bertrand Aristide, Haiti's first democratically elected president. The United States, while advocating democracy, was accused of tacitly supporting the coup and its perpetrators, unleashing a wave of repression that sent thousands of Haitians fleeing once again.

Economic crises, combined with chronic political instability, forced many families to take to the sea in makeshift boats, hoping to reach American shores. In response, the United States has implemented restrictive migration policies, such as interceptions at sea and the systematic return of boats to Haiti or to detention centers in Guantanamo. This has only worsened the situation of Haitian refugees, who are caught in a cycle of hope and disillusionment, often the victims of political decisions made in Washington.

Fourth wave: the economic crisis and the 2010 earthquake

The devastating earthquake of January 2010 marked another critical milestone in the history of Haitian immigration to the United States. One of the deadliest earthquakes in recent history, it killed more than 200,000 people and left millions homeless, worsening an already ailing economy. Although the United States sent immediate humanitarian aid, the long-term response was characterized by clumsy interventions and aid that did not always meet needs. At the same time, tens of thousands of Haitians were allowed to immigrate temporarily under a Temporary Protected Status (TPS) program, but this status remained precarious and under constant threat of deportation with each administration.

As the Haitian economy deteriorated and insecurity increased, many Haitians attempted to reach the United States by taking dangerous routes through the Latin American country, creating a protracted migration crisis. American policy remained contradictory, oscillating between temporary compassion and systematic repression.

Fifth wave: the current political and security crisis

Today, Haiti faces one of the worst security and political crises in its history. Since the assassination of President Jovenel Moïse on the night of July 7-8, 2021, the country has been plunged into chaos, with armed gangs controlling large areas of the capital, Port-au-Prince. While the United States claims to want to stabilize Haiti, it remains partly responsible for the country's institutional collapse by supporting corrupt and ineffective governments for decades. This new wave of instability has led to an increase in mass emigration, with many Haitians seeking to escape violence and misery by attempting to reach the United States.

Once again, U.S. policy has vacillated between limited humanitarian admissions and border closures, creating a climate of uncertainty for those trying to flee. This latest wave of Haitian immigration reflects not only the failure of Haiti's domestic policies, but also the failure of international interventions, particularly American, that have allowed a once prosperous country to descend into chaos.

Each wave of Haitian immigration to the United States reflects a deep crisis exacerbated by decades of U.S. political, economic, and military interference in Haiti. As Haitians flee poverty, violence, and instability, they are often caught up in restrictive U.S. migration policies that oscillate between selective admission and repression. The United States, seeking to preserve its strategic interests in the region, has helped create these crises, creating a cycle of forced migration that generations of Haitians have had to endure.

This wave of Haitian immigration seems to mark a decisive turning point in the history of migration between Haiti and the United States. While thousands of Haitian families are still torn apart by the socio-political crisis, economic instability, and natural disasters that rocked their country, President Joe Biden's administration has introduced a ray of hope: the "humanitarian parole" program. Designed to provide a legal and temporary pathway for migrants facing hardship in their home countries, this program could be a lifeline for this new generation of Haitian immigrants.

Since January 2023, this initiative has taken on a special dimension. Haitians, along with nationals of Cuba, Venezuela and Nicaragua, have been identified as priorities for obtaining this "humanitarian word". For many, this is not just a migration policy measure, but a concrete opportunity to escape the violence, poverty and instability ravaging Haiti. The program allows up to 30,000 people a month to enter the U.S. legally, provided they have sponsors who agree to support them financially. These sponsors, often family members already established in the United States, are essential to ensuring that new arrivals can begin a more stable life in America.

For this fifth wave of Haitians, the program is a lifeline. Unlike previous waves, who often had to make dangerous sea crossings or apply for asylum in precarious conditions, these new arrivals benefit from a more secure environment. The conditions for admission are clear: beneficiaries must apply from abroad and receive authorization before entering the country.

This avoids the suffering that many illegal immigrants have endured in the past.

But this fifth wave is not without its challenges. Officially, the program has just ended. This means that although these Haitians have escaped the hell of Haiti, they face the hell of discrimination and racism, especially in Springfield; they already know their return date: January 2024.

Nevertheless, this new wave of Haitian immigrants has arrived in a context where the Haitian diaspora has already established a strong presence in the United States. Haitians in Florida, New York, and Boston, among other places, are well integrated into the economic and cultural fabric of the country. Thanks to community solidarity and a network of family support, many are able to stabilize and rebuild their lives by changing their status.

CHAPTER TWO

CONSCIENCE THAT THE ACT OF MIGRATION IS NOT DEHUMANIZING

If there are silly jobs for some in Haiti, the first advice the Haitian immigrant in the United States gives you is not to learn the language, it's not to go to school, it's to go to work, and there are no considerations. No job is ever too bad; he tells you that work is freedom. Incomprehensible at first, but it's a truth that quickly catches up with you. I had just finished studying political marketing in Rome and arrived in the country that created political marketing, the option of any job was not on the table, and yet. After sending out resumes and applying for dozens of jobs without success, I had to follow the advice of my old classmate. So, with my master's degree, my first job, albeit a very short one, was chauffeuring pilots and flight attendants to their hotels and the airport. The lesson in all of this is that no honorable job dehumanizes you, it's the fact of living at the expense of others; not being able to take care of your own needs that dehumanizes you. And getting that job where it's at, so that your children's lives depend on you alone, is honorable.

Since the beginning of time, people have sought to cross borders, explore unknown lands, to settle where the hope of a better life seemed more tangible. This quest continues today. Every year, millions of people leave their homes, leaving behind everything they've ever known: their family, their culture, their language, their memories. For most, this departure is an act of courage, an attempt to survive, a gamble on the future. But what drives a person to leave everything behind and head into the unknown? What sacrifices are required to build a new life elsewhere? What impact do these decisions have on the identity and well-being of those who make them? More human before, less human after?

The act of migration is not dehumanizing. On the contrary, it is a powerful testament to resilience, the pursuit of dignity, and the fundamental desire of every human being to live in a safe, free, and prosperous environment. Those who migrate, whether forced by war, poverty, natural disaster, or political persecution, do not renounce their humanity by crossing borders. They powerfully affirm it.

History shows us that migration is inextricably linked to human nature. Since the dawn of humanity, people have been on the move, whether in search of better land, new opportunities, or simply to survive. This constant movement has never caused individuals to lose their humanity; on the contrary, it has enriched cultures, built civilizations, and fostered the human exchanges that are at the root of the diversity and richness of the modern world. To think that migration is dehumanizing is to deny this historical and social reality.

When we talk about migration, we must remember that behind every number, every policy, every border, there are human beings with unique stories, dreams, families, and hopes. The idea that crossing a border diminishes the value of a human being is a false construct often used to justify exclusionary policies. The migrant remains a human being with inalienable rights, whether in his or her country of origin or in a foreign country.

The process of migration is too often reduced to a simple loss. We hear of the loss of roots, landmarks and social status. We hear painful stories of exile, of forced alienation from one's homeland, of the gradual erasure of memories that fade with time. This vision, while not entirely false, remains incomplete. It lacks a fundamental element: migration is an act of courage. It is the manifestation of an inner strength that refuses to be crushed by circumstances. It's a search for dignity, survival, and often prosperity under adverse conditions.

To migrate is to take control of one's destiny with unwavering determination where others would have given up. It's about freeing yourself from a context that leaves you no choice but to seek an opportunity to live life to the full elsewhere. Leaving one's roots is certainly painful, but it's also a gesture of revolt against a situation that prevents fulfillment. It's saying no to fate.

Migration is therefore not an act of dehumanization, but rather a manifestation of an individual's inner strength in the face of adversity. By migrating, individuals are exercising their fundamental right to seek a better future for themselves and their loved ones. This does not diminish their humanity; it enhances it. It is important not to reduce migrants to numbers or dehumanizing stereotypes.

It is our collective duty to recognize their dignity and to understand that, like all human beings, they simply seek to live in conditions that respect their dignity and integrity.

The current debate on migration, especially in developed countries, is often fraught with fear, xenophobia and preconceived notions. Yet migration is a natural response to global inequalities, conflicts and climate change. Migrants are not "others" alien to our humanity; they are men, women and children who, like all of us, seek a better life.

It is crucial to put the human being back at the center of the migration debate. We must refuse to give in to discourses that dehumanize migrants by presenting them as a threat or a burden. On the contrary, we must adopt a vision that recognizes immigration as a phenomenon inextricably linked to humanity and its history. Today's migrations, like those of the past, contribute to building more open, resilient, and prosperous societies. This is part of the human condition, and it is something we must recognize and defend.

Humanity in motivation

Today, as we watch the increasing harassment of Haitian immigrants in the United States, we can't help but feel a deep sense of injustice and revolt. It's as if the very existence of Haitians is being questioned, as if we as a people have lost the basic right to live. The right to be human on this earth, with our hopes, dreams and aspirations, seems to be trampled underfoot. These men, women and children fleeing misery, violence and instability in search of a better life are treated as intruders, as undesirables. Their suffering and pain are invisible to those who close doors, who build walls instead of reaching out.

But Haitian immigration is not a threat. It reflects the resilience of a people who refuse to give up. Every Haitian who sets foot on American soil, hoping to find refuge and dignity, is only looking for a chance to live in peace, to contribute to society, to build a future for their children. They are mothers, fathers, brothers and sisters, all driven by the hope of a better tomorrow. They flee not by choice, but by necessity, because life at home has become unbearable. Who can blame them for simply wanting to exist, for wanting to be treated with dignity and humanity? How can we turn a blind eye to the plight of a people whose only desire is to survive?

This inhumane treatment not only undermines the dignity of Haitians, it undermines humanity as a whole. By rejecting these immigrants, by depriving them of their right to live in peace, we betray the very values on which the

United States was built: liberty, equality, and justice for all. Every act of rejection, every expulsion, is a wound inflicted on the ideal of human brotherhood.

Haitians are not asking for charity. They are asking for justice. They are asking to be treated as human beings with rights, aspirations and dreams. They have contributed and continue to contribute to American society through their work, their culture, and their resilience. They deserve to be welcomed, not rejected. They deserve to be recognized, reached out to, and given their rightful place in the country they have chosen to rebuild their lives.

It's time to wake up and look at these men and women with compassionate eyes. It's time to say stop the relentlessness, stop the dehumanization. It's not just about immigration, it's about our humanity. What kind of world do we want to build? A world of rejection, of hatred, of closure? Or a world of openness, of solidarity, where every human being has the right to live in dignity, regardless of his or her background? It's not just the future of Haitians that is at stake, it's the future of all humanity.

Every crisis in the country brings its share of migrants, and over time the motivations are the same.

A. – Exploring motivations: poverty, war, persecution, and hope for a better life

Although in my case, insecurity led us to the exit door, the reasons that drive people to leave their country are many and complex. While each story is unique, certain themes recur persistently in migrants' accounts.

Poverty: Escape from misery

For many, the exodus is motivated by the need to survive. Poverty, with its consequences of lack of opportunity, hunger, lack of health care, and limited access to education, is a powerful driver of immigration. Statistics show that in developing countries a large proportion of the population lives on less than two dollars a day. Under these conditions, it is almost impossible to imagine a stable future for oneself and one's family.

A Haitian farmer, for example, whose crops are relentlessly destroyed by tropical storms, faces an unrelenting reality. Year after year, the fruits of his labor are swept away by winds, torrential rains, and floods. Despite his best efforts, he comes to the painful conclusion that he will never be able to support his family by staying in his home country. What was once his hope, his inheritance became a dead end in which despair takes root.

For this man, immigration becomes more than an option; it's a necessity. It's the only chance he sees to change the destiny of his children, to give them what he never had: access to education, decent medical care, a life of dignity, far from the uncertainties that punctuate his daily life. He doesn't dream of wealth or luxury, but of giving his children the chance to live with dignity, without the constant fear of the next storm or the next crop failure.

It's with this hope in mind that thousands of men and women, like this farmer, make a heartbreaking decision every year: to leave their land, their family, their roots, and everything that makes up their identity, to venture into the unknown. They know that the journey is perilous, that they risk their lives crossing stormy seas in makeshift boats or crossing unforgiving deserts. But faced with the alternative of a hopeless future, they choose to risk everything to give their children a chance, however small, at prosperity and peace.

These migrants are not motivated by a thirst for adventure or comfort. Their decision is neither light nor reckless; it is the fruit of long reflection, of a vital need to survive. Behind each departure is a story of sacrifice, renunciation, suffering, and exaggerated hopes. They do not flee on a whim, but because they know that the future they hope for their children can never be realized in a country where nature and political instability combine to destroy their dreams season after season.

How can we remain indifferent in the face of these realities? How can we, in our affluent societies, fail to understand that for these men and women, immigration is much more than a simple geographical displacement? It's a search for dignity, a fierce determination to break free from a fate that seems inevitable. By seeking refuge elsewhere, they are trying above all to save their humanity, to protect what is most precious to them: their children, their families, and their future.

The risks they take to leave their homes are a testament to their courage and determination. They don't come to beg; they come to build, to contribute, to participate in the construction of a better world, not only for themselves, but for all of us. After all, their struggle for survival and dignity is a constant reminder of the fragility of our own lives and of the importance of solidarity and welcoming others.

Every migrant who crosses our borders, with his or her dreams and fears, holds up a mirror to us: an invitation to reflect on what it truly means to be human. Will we welcome them as brothers and sisters, recognizing their courage and resilience? Or will we reject them, turning a blind eye to their suffering, to their basic need to survive and live with dignity?

Immigration is not a burden, it's a promise. A promise of the future, of renewal, of shared prosperity. It is our duty not to forget this, not to betray these men and women who, against all odds, choose to believe in a better future for their children.

War and insecurity: the search for peace

For others, exile is a matter of life and death. Armed conflicts, civil wars, and state violence force millions of people to flee their homes every year. These people leave not because they want to, but because they have no choice. Syria, Sudan, Afghanistan, the Democratic Republic of Congo, and many other countries have seen their populations scattered to the four corners of the globe to escape bombs, militias, and violence.

When war destroys everything that constitutes a stable existence - the home that sheltered memories, the job that fed the family, the schools where children dreamed of a future, the hospitals that cared for sick bodies - there's nothing left. Nothing but chaos, fear, and uncertainty. In the face of this collapse, leaving becomes the only option, the only hope of survival.

For these men, women, and often children, exile is not a choice, but a necessity imposed by the brutality of the world. They flee not out of a desire for adventure, but because to stay is to die. Each stage of their journey is a relentless battle against the forces that seek to destroy them. They march through hostile territory where any detour can lead to death, where danger is synonymous with unscrupulous smugglers waiting to exploit, deceive and abandon them.

The nights are cold and full of nightmares. During the day, the oppressive heat wears them down, but they keep going, driven by an inner strength they never knew they had. Some must cross stormy seas on makeshift boats as fragile as their hopes. Every wave that hits these fragile boats seems to remind them that life can change at any moment. Children's cries echo, mothers' tears mingle with the salt water, and yet they hang on.

For them, arriving alive in a safe country, setting foot in a land where war does not dictate the laws, where bombs do not fall from the sky, is already a victory. It's the fruit of their courage, their resilience, and their inextinguishable will to survive even when all seems lost. Their hearts beat faster, not in fear this time, but in relief. They are here. Alive. After so much toil, so many sacrifices.

Although physical survival is assured, another struggle begins: that for dignity, recognition, for integration into a world that often looks at them with suspicion, even hostility. They are no longer just victims of war, but "migrants", a word full of prejudice, a word that in many societies has become synonymous with a threat.

Yet these men and women are much more than "migrants". They are survivors, silent heroes who have defied death to give their children a chance at life. They carry with them stories of suffering, but also of courage, hope, and unbreakable dreams. They bring cultures, languages, and knowledge that enrich the countries that welcome them if those countries know how to welcome them with humanity.

How can we deny them their rightful place? In the face of such resilience, how can we treat them as unwanted strangers, as burdens? Every life saved is a victory for humanity. Every migrant who manages to cross the borders of a safe country is a living testament to our ability as a species to overcome the inhuman, protect life, and build bridges across differences and fears.

So, yes, just arriving alive in a safe country is a victory for them. But that should not be the end of their story. That victory deserves to be honored, extended by a dignified welcome, a recognition of their humanity and courage. These men and women are not intruders in our societies; they are potential builders, the bearers of the future. The journey they have undertaken is undeniable proof of the strength of the human desire to live and to protect those close to us.

And by opening our doors to them, by offering them the chance to rebuild their lives on new foundations, we also affirm our own humanity. We recognize that the act of migration is not a weakness, but an act of courage. An act that deserves not only our respect but also our solidarity. Because in the end, every migrant who survives reminds us of ourselves, of what we hold most precious: the instinct to survive, the desire to protect our children, the hope for a better future.

Persecution: fleeing injustice

In addition to war, other forms of violence and persecution drive people into exile. In many countries, people are persecuted because of their ethnicity, religion or sexual orientation. Being born with an identity different from the dominant norm can be enough to turn a life into hell. Afghan women who refuse to submit to the strict rules of the Taliban, oppressed ethnic minorities in Burma, or homosexuals in Iran often have no choice but to flee for their lives.

These people seek not only physical refuge but also a place where they can be themselves without fear of reprisal. They flee so that they can live out their identities, their beliefs, and their loves, with dignity and freedom. For them, immigration is not a choice, but a necessity.

The hope of a better life: the dream of opportunity

There are also those who leave, not because they are driven by fear or misery, but because they are attracted by the hope of a better future. These migrants are not fleeing immediate danger, but are seeking to improve their quality of life, to realize dreams that their home country cannot offer. America, Europe, and Australia, for example, represent to them lands of opportunity, where hard work is rewarded, where it's possible to start a business, pursue higher education, and live a more fulfilling life.

This hope for a better life is often fueled by the stories of those who have already left and who, despite the difficulties, manage to send money home to their families, build a house, and pay for the education of their brothers and sisters back home. For many, these success stories are tangible proof that despite the sacrifices, the game is worth the candle.

B. – Testimonies and Personal Experiences

Nothing illustrates the reality of immigration like the stories of those who have experienced it. These stories reflect the diversity of experiences and reasons for leaving home.

Jean, 34, Haiti

Jean left Haiti after the devastating 2010 earthquake. His home was destroyed, and his family was living in precarious conditions in a refugee camp. At that point, I told myself I had to leave," he recalls. "I couldn't let my children grow up in a place where there was no school, no hospital, no future." Jean borrowed money from relatives to pay a smuggler who took him to the U.S. border. "After several months of travel, I risked my life, but I had no choice. Today I work as a laborer. It's hard, but I can send money to my family, and I hope that one day we will all be reunited here."

Amina, 28, Syria

Amina left Syria in 2015 after her village was targeted by bombs. "I saw friends die in front of my eyes," she confides. "We ran out of food and water. We had to leave or die." She and her two-year-old son crossed the Mediterranean in a makeshift boat. "I was scared the whole way. I didn't know if we would survive." Today she lives in Germany, where she is learning the language and hopes to become a nurse. "I miss Syria, but I want to give my son a future. Here he can go to school, he's safe. That's all that matters."

Carlos, 42, Honduras

Carlos left Honduras to escape the gangs that were threatening his family. "I owned a small grocery store. One day, some gang members came to me and asked for money. I gave them everything I had, but they said it wasn't enough. I knew they would kill me if I stayed. Carlos closed his business and left for the United States with his wife and two children. "The trip was a nightmare. We walked for days without food, not knowing if we would make it." Today, he lives in Los Angeles, where he works as a security guard. "It's not the life I imagined, but we're safe, and that's all that matters."

These testimonies show that immigration is never an easy choice. It's an act of survival, resistance, and courage. For every migrant, departure is a turning point, a painful separation from all that is familiar. It's a leap into the unknown, a risky gamble on the future.

We heard from Ukrainians who fled their country and Palestinians who left Gaza. These are heartbreaking stories of forced exile, hasty goodbyes, and shattered dreams. They are stories that illustrate human suffering, but also the indomitable hope to survive and one day find a life of dignity, free from fear and violence.

Testimonies of Ukrainians:

Irina, a mother of two, had to leave Kyiv at the beginning of the invasion. She recounts the heartbreak of this forced departure:

"I will never forget that morning. The sky was dark, explosions shook the windows. I grabbed my children, took a bag with some clothes and our passports. That was all. In a few minutes we left our home, our life. My husband stayed behind to fight, and I left, alone with our children, not knowing where we were going or when we'd be back. Every kilometer we walked was another step away from what we knew, our home, our roots. I felt my heart breaking a little more every day."

Irina's words reveal the pain of heartbreaking separation, of those millions of Ukrainian families torn apart by war. And yet, through it all, she stands firm, for her children, to give them a chance to escape the horror.

Pavlo, a student from Kharkiv, recalls his hasty departure in the middle of the night: "We had heard the sirens all day. Bombs were falling all around us. I decided to leave when a rocket destroyed the building next door. I had 10 minutes to get my things together. I took nothing but my laptop and some books. I fled without looking back, my heart heavy from leaving behind everything I'd known. But I had no choice. I could have died if I'd stayed."

Testimonies of Palestinians in Gaza:

Fatima, a mother of three, left Gaza with her family after years of blockade and repeated bombardment: "Living in Gaza is like living in an open-air prison. Every day we lived in fear of bombs, air raids, and bullets. I still remember the sound of planes flying over our house, day and night. The children were crying, terrified. We had nowhere to run. We decided to leave when our house was partially destroyed in a strike. Leaving Gaza was like giving up a part of my soul. But I could no longer see my children growing up in such a nightmare."

Fatima's words bear witness to the daily anguish of Gaza, a territory marked by war and misery, where the inhabitants live in a constant struggle for survival. For Fatima and so many others, leaving was the only option to give their children a chance at life.

Ahmad, a young man of 24, remembers leaving Gaza:

"Leaving was one of the most difficult decisions of my life. I didn't want to leave my family, my friends, my country. But there was no future for me in Gaza. No jobs, no freedom. There was destruction, death, and suffering everywhere. I crossed borders, and walked through the desert, all to find a better life. I didn't know if I would find it, but I had to try."

Like so many young Palestinians, Ahmad left Gaza not because he wanted to, but because staying meant giving up all hope. His departure symbolizes a final act of resistance: the search for a life where he can exist without the constant threat of violence.

These poignant stories, whether from Ukraine or Gaza, share a universal pain: that of families torn apart, lands abandoned, hopes suspended. These testimonies are not just stories of exile but cries from the heart, appeals to humanity. They remind us that behind every immigrant, behind every refugee, there is a human being yearning for peace, dignity and a better future.

Their courage and strength in the face of adversity are living testaments to human resilience. These men, women, and children fleeing war and oppression deserve our solidarity and support. They are not just numbers or anonymous waves of immigrants. They are people with stories, dreams, and a fierce will to live in the face of adversity.

Through their testimonies, we see that even in the most terrible circumstances, hope remains. And this hope, this call for solidarity, is a responsibility we cannot ignore. Because behind every story of escape, there is a struggle for survival, and behind every struggle, there is a life that deserves to be protected and respected.

C. – Leaving Behind: Family, Culture, Identity

One of the most heartbreaking aspects of immigration is undoubtedly the sacrifice of all that is familiar. Leaving one's home is much more than a simple journey to an unknown land; it's uprooting. It's saying goodbye, often with no guarantee of return, to everything that makes up our existence: family, friends, the language we've spoken since childhood, the culture that has shaped our identity. It means leaving behind the landscapes where we grew up, the alleys where we played as children, the traditions that give rhythm and meaning to our daily lives.

By tearing himself away from all this, the immigrant cuts himself off from his roots, his landmarks, and his past. He sets out into the unknown, certain only of what he's leaving behind, unsure of what awaits him on the other side. Every step he takes him a little further away from what made him who he is. It's not just a geographical exile, but an inner one, a deep, intimate rupture that leaves its mark forever.

Leaving also means facing overwhelming loneliness. Our mother tongue, the language in which we dream, cry and laugh, suddenly becomes foreign to those around us. Every conversation is an effort, every word a struggle to express ourselves in a language that is not our own. Customs that were once so natural, become incomprehensible, and what seemed obvious becomes complex. It's living in a world where you no longer recognize anything, where even after years you still feel out of step, still a stranger.

This sacrifice, the sacrifice of all that is familiar, is an immense price to pay. But in spite of all this, immigrants continue to leave, hoping for a better future. They carry their roots in their hearts, trying to rebuild, to reinvent a home in a new land. But the sense of loss is always there, like an invisible scar. Immigration is an act of courage, but also an act of renunciation, a sacrifice that leaves no one untouched.

Family: the absence of loved ones

Leaving one's family behind is perhaps the greatest sacrifice an immigrant can make. The absence of loved ones is an open wound, a dull pain that inhabits every moment, an immense void that nothing can fill. Modern technology allows us to see faces and hear voices, but these video calls, no matter how frequent, will never replace the warmth of a real hug, the reassuring feeling of being next to those we love. What's still missing is that physical closeness, that human contact that alone can soothe the soul.

For parents who leave their children behind, the pain takes on an even more unbearable dimension. Every day away from their children is a lost day, a moment stolen by distance, a day of birthdays, first steps, and small moments of family happiness that will never return. Every smile seen through a screen is a cruel reminder of the impossibility of sharing that moment together, in the same room. And although these sacrifices are made to give their children a better future, the pain of not seeing them grow up is overwhelming.

Those who leave their homeland with the promise of one day being reunited with their family live with this constant pain, the pain of a heart divided between two worlds. They move forward with the tenacious hope of one day being reunited with their loved ones while carrying the weight of that absence, that lack that makes every success in a foreign land bitter. This sacrifice, invisible to many, is the most profound. Behind every immigrant's face is a story of love, separation, hope, and silent tears shed in anticipation of reunion.

Many migrants go years, even decades, without seeing their loved ones. Some never see them again. This is the price of exile: enforced loneliness, a constant feeling of being uprooted and torn apart.

Culture: the loss of self

Leaving is more than a physical move. It means giving up part of yourself, leaving behind essential parts of your identity. Living far from home means finding yourself in a world where everything is different: language, customs, landscapes, and familiar smells that remind us of our childhood. It's a world where even the tastes of food seem foreign, where the taste of childhood becomes a distant memory.

For many immigrants, this cultural break is a painful ordeal. The simple fact of no longer hearing their mother tongue echo in the streets, sharing the expressions that made people smile, tasting the traditional dishes that warmed the soul, all contribute to a profound sense of loss. The feasts and celebrations that once marked the rhythm of life have become solitary moments or shared from afar, through a screen, in a desperate attempt to recreate the atmosphere of yesteryear.

This separation, this distance from one's cultural roots, creates a feeling of alienation. One becomes a stranger, not only to a foreign country but sometimes to oneself. Nostalgia becomes a faithful companion, this irrepressible longing to rediscover the little things that made everyday life so beautiful in one's native land. But this return to one's roots is often impossible. We're caught between two worlds, neither quite here nor quite there.

And yet, despite this loss, there is always the strength to recreate, to rebuild. Immigrants reinvent their traditions in this new world, using the cuisine of their childhood as a bridge to their past, passing on their culture to their children, even thousands of miles away. But this process never completely erases the wound. Uprooting leaves deep traces, a permanent melancholy, but also the strength to have survived this rupture.

For first-generation immigrants, preserving culture is a constant challenge. They strive to pass on to their children the traditions, language, and values they consider essential, while at the same time adapting to a new environment. The risk is to see these elements wither away, to feel betrayed by a world that does not recognize their heritage.

Identity: rebuilding elsewhere

Ultimately, immigration is above all a process of reinvention. It's a journey of trials, of learning to see yourself in a new light, of redefining who you are. Immigrants must juggle multiple identities, adapt to unfamiliar norms, and meet expectations that are different from those of their country of origin. This process is often painful and requires compromises, concessions, and sometimes even the abandonment of certain facets of oneself in order to integrate or simply survive.

It's not just about mastering a new language or understanding the customs and practices of a new country. It's also about taking on different roles, sometimes less rewarding than the ones you had at home. Doctors become taxi drivers; engineers work as laborers. All at the cost of immense personal sacrifice. It means giving up part of one's history, one's achievements, in order to adapt to a different, often unforgiving reality.

Immigrating also means learning to face the way others see you, overcoming prejudices, and fighting exclusion. It means proving yourself in a world that doesn't expect you to, and that doesn't always make things easy for you. For many, it's a daily existence in which the feeling of being an outsider persists, despite the efforts, despite the years spent trying to find one's place.

But this reinvention, however difficult, is also a form of resilience. It demonstrates the human capacity to adapt, to open oneself to the unknown, to overcome obstacles. Every immigrant who successfully makes his or her way in a new country demonstrates that identity is fluid, and we can redefine ourselves without denying our roots. It's an act of survival, of course, but it's also an act of creation and transformation.

There is great strength in this quest. Despite hardship, despite loss, the immigrant never stops dreaming of a better future. He reinvents himself for himself, but also for his children, for the next generation. This process, though difficult, is a source of hope. It reminds us that even in the darkest moments it is always possible to rebuild, to be reborn in a new, stronger, more resilient form.

Immigration, then, is not simply a renunciation. It's also an opportunity for growth, an ordeal that forges a new self. It's a powerful demonstration of man's ability to reinvent himself in the face of obstacles, to pick himself up, and move forward with courage and determination.

But this reconstruction of identity can also be a source of strength and resilience. The immigrant learns to navigate between two worlds, blending the best of each culture to create a new identity. It's a process that, while difficult, can lead to greater openness, inner richness, and the ability to see the world through new eyes. In the late 1970s, a large number of Haitians settled in the Miami area, revitalizing the community of Lemon City, which became known as "Little Haiti. The name was coined by Haitian businessman and community leader Viter Juste, who saw the emerging neighborhood as a reflection of the Haitian capital, Port-au-Prince. The culturally vibrant Haitian community would enrich Miami-Dade County with its multi-ethnic character and infuse it with the traditions and customs of their homeland.

immigration as an act of faith

Leaving one's country is an act of faith, a bold step into the unknown. It's a decision that goes beyond a simple desire for change: it's a search for dignity, an attempt to reclaim what seems to be slipping away. There are many reasons why a person might decide to leave everything behind, but they all coalesce around a common sentiment: hope.

The hope of escaping misery, of escaping the clutches of violence or relentless persecution. Hope to build a life where the future is not clouded by fear or despair. The hope of seeing their children grow up in an environment where their talents are recognized, where they have access to quality education, to medical care, a future where anything still seems possible.

It's this almost palpable hope that drives millions of people every year to cross borders, to brave scorching deserts, to cross raging oceans. The risks are enormous, the dangers real, but faced with a life without prospects, without a future, the choice seems almost natural. The fear of standing still becomes greater than the fear of the unknown.

But immigration is not simply an act of survival. It is above all a search for dignity. For in the soul of every migrant is the profound human desire to live in freedom, no longer bound by the chains of poverty or oppression. It's a cry from the heart, a fierce desire to regain control of one's destiny, to offer one's loved ones a life in which they can flourish.

Leaving is also about faith. Believing that a better life is possible across borders, walls, and oceans. To believe that every ordeal along the way - the dangerous crossing, the administrative hurdles, the racism, or marginalization - will be worth it in the end. This hope is often the only thing that remains, the only engine that keeps us going, that keeps us from giving up.

Hope is what gives us the strength to walk for days in extreme conditions, to trust unscrupulous smugglers, to risk everything for an uncertain future. It is this hope that keeps migrants going despite the difficulties. They find the strength to rebuild, to integrate, to contribute to their new society, in the hope that their sacrifices will enable their children to live a better life.

This act of faith, this unshakable hope, is at the heart of every immigration story. It is the light that guides those who decide to leave everything behind. It is that despite obstacles and injustices, human beings remain capable of dreaming, believing, and fighting for a dignified and just future. In the end, leaving one's country is much more than a physical journey. It's an inner adventure, a search for oneself, a reaffirmation of the intrinsic value of every human being: that of deserving a better life.

CHAPTER THREE

CONSCIENCE OF THE CHALLENGES OF INTEGRATION

In my culture, living on credit is frowned upon. You pay cash for everything, you pay the whole amount at once, and that inspires respect. It's a badge of honor. So, when I first arrived, I couldn't understand how Americans could live permanently under the yoke of credit. It was a real shock to me to discover that if you don't have credit, you're practically shut out of the system. To rent an apartment: credit. To buy a car: credit. Everything goes through this invisible but omnipresent lever.

It took me a long time, and several mistakes, to finally understand that in this society, credit is the true measure of respectability. It was unthinkable to me. In my culture, being in debt is a shame, a disgraceful burden. Here, having debt is seen as a sign of responsibility, as long as you make the minimum payment on time.

It's as if credit defines the value of your life. You never really own what you have; you're constantly borrowing to exist, to stay afloat in a never-ending race. Working endlessly becomes a necessity, not to live in the present, but to pay off the debts accumulated by living beyond one's means. This model, so far removed from my points of reference, made me realize the extent to which our cultures have been shaped by opposing notions of respect and honor.

But it's a key element in getting into the great American society.

You can understand that arriving in a new country is both an exhilarating and terrifying experience. For an immigrant, every step on foreign soil is both a victory and a leap into the unknown. Everything is new: the faces, the buildings, the customs. It's like entering a parallel universe where every detail is both familiar and strange. Behind the excitement of starting a new life lies a whirlwind of challenges and uncertainties. How do you integrate into a society you know so little about? How do you understand and respect social norms, values, and laws that can sometimes seem confusing? How do you navigate a world where the language, climate, and even the food is different? In this chapter, we explore the culture shock immigrants feel, their first impressions of American society, and the many practical obstacles they must overcome to integrate and build a new life.

A. – Culture Shock: Discovering New Laws, Social Norms, and Value Systems

Culture shock is an intimate, profound ordeal that strikes at the core of a person's identity. Imagine an entire life built on values, traditions, and social codes that suddenly make no sense in a new environment. This feeling of disorientation, even vertigo, occurs when the immigrant is plunged into a society with reference points that are completely different from his or her own. This culture shock, well documented by sociologists and psychologists, is often invisible to the naked eye, but no less devastating.

For those who have left everything behind, adaptation becomes an internal struggle. People think that immigrating is simply changing the country, but it's also changing the world. What was normal, what was part of the daily routine, suddenly becomes strange, almost incomprehensible. Sometimes it's the simplest gestures, such as saying hello, eating at the table or getting dressed, that remind the immigrant that he or she is no longer at home.

This sudden confrontation with different habits, beliefs, and behaviors can shatter ingrained certainties and leave the immigrant in a state of extreme vulnerability. He or she must relearn how to live, how to decipher the signs of a new culture, and how to develop linguistic subtleties that still elude them. It's a process that often erodes self-esteem, because it's not just a matter of adapting, but of facing the reality of feeling like a stranger in a world where everything seemed accessible in dreams.

Culture shock is not just a matter of practical adjustment. It's also an existential question: Who am I when I'm no longer in my own environment? Rituals that once marked important moments in life - family celebrations, religious observances, local customs - suddenly seem distant, almost inaccessible. The immigrant must juggle two worlds: that of his past, which he tries to keep alive in his heart, and that of his present, which he must master in order to survive.

This shock is sometimes so intense that it leads to a feeling of isolation. Feeling misunderstood, coming up against invisible walls, being confronted with racism or indifference only reinforces this feeling of being a foreigner, even in the most everyday places. Every glance, every word can become an additional ordeal, a reminder that the road to integration is long and difficult.

But there's a paradoxical power in this culture shock. For every immigrant who manages to overcome this shock, there is a victory: that of human resilience. Behind the pain, the confusion, the loneliness, there's a heart that adapts, a mind that refuses to give up, a person who finds in himself a new capacity to open up, to learn, to grow.

This culture shock, as intense as it is, also becomes a bridge. With time, the immigrant discovers how to navigate between the two worlds, how to integrate the best of the new culture while preserving the treasures of his heritage. This transformation, this painful but necessary process, allows the immigrant to rediscover an unsuspected strength: that of being both a product of his original culture and a full-fledged player in his new society.

In my particular case, when I landed in Florida, after the warm welcome of all my family who immigrated in the 80s, within an hour I was in contact with other Haitian immigrants, former classmates, former colleagues, friends, and so on. It was like being in Haiti, I felt it intensely because I was from Italy. Indeed, for a Haitian, the culture shock in the United States has a singularity that distinguishes it from that experienced in other countries. Here, in the heart of this vast and diverse country, the immigrant has the rare and precious opportunity to find a piece of home in this elsewhere. When he arrives on American soil, he is not alone. He discovers, sometimes with relief, entire communities who, like him, have left their homelands and brought their traditions, language, and customs with them. This strong connection to his native culture becomes a lifeline in an ocean of the unknown.

Unlike many destinations where cultural isolation can be total, as it was for me in Italy, the U.S. offers newcomers the opportunity to rely on a network of compatriots. This provides invaluable moral support. When faced with a language barrier, unfamiliar customs, and a seemingly alien environment, knowing that you can find a corner of your country in a neighborhood, an association, or a place of worship soothes the brutal shock.

These immigrant communities play a crucial role in integration. They allow us to find our bearings, to reconnect with familiar tastes, to share similar stories and similar journeys into exile. These encounters remind us that we're not alone in our ordeal. It's a human warmth that soothes, restores hope and encourages us to persevere.

This community presence keeps alive traditions, festivals and rituals that might otherwise be lost in the hardships of daily life. It becomes a refuge where you can speak your mother tongue without fear, where you can share a traditional meal without bitter nostalgia. Most of all, it's a place where you can express your fears and doubts without being judged.

The United States, with its history of immigration, is a crossroads of cultures. This doesn't mean that culture shock doesn't exist - far from it. It's always there, powerful, disorienting, and challenging. But it is mitigated by the opportunity to meet those who have already made the journey, who have already faced and overcome these challenges, and who are there to share their experiences, to advise, to listen.

This network of support is not limited to ethnic communities. Many organizations, whether religious, social or cultural, work to integrate immigrants. They offer resources, language courses and employment assistance, but above all they reach out to those who are trying to rebuild their lives in the turmoil of exile. This makes it easier to navigate this complex society, to acquire the tools needed to overcome obstacles and, above all, to avoid feeling overwhelmed by the immensity of change.

Of course, the road ahead remains difficult. Culture shock doesn't disappear overnight. It takes time to understand and come to terms with this new reality. But thanks to the presence of other immigrants, thanks to this solidarity that transcends borders, integration becomes a journey you don't have to take alone. And therein lies America's true strength: in its ability to welcome those who arrive with their baggage, their dreams and their hopes, and to offer them a chance to put down roots while retaining a piece of their heritage.

In the process, each immigrant discovers himself to be stronger, more resilient. They learn to reconcile their past with their future, to preserve their identity while embracing that of their new country. And this journey, though arduous, is also a source of immeasurable richness, both for the immigrant and for the host society.

Discovering new laws

An immigrant's first encounter with his or her new country inevitably involves discovering its laws, and this moment can be both intimidating and enlightening. A country's laws are not just rules to be followed; they reflect its deepest values, its sense of justice, what it considers fair and necessary to organize life in society. Every article, every rule is imbued with a history, a culture, a way of understanding good and evil, freedom and responsibility.

For an immigrant, this encounter with the legal system is often the first step in understanding a society that is foreign to him. It's a new language to decipher, a framework to respect, but also a space where they can feel protected and recognized. Laws define what he can do, how he can fit in, but also the rights he is granted, the protection he is offered. They are a compass that guides his first steps in this unknown land, and sometimes they are the only bulwark against injustice and arbitrariness.

However, this discovery is not without difficulties. The laws can seem complex, rigid, and incomprehensible. They remind us that the immigrant is still a stranger in this new environment. But at the same time, they offer an opportunity to understand how a society based on principles works, to find one's place in a system that, despite its imperfections, guarantees rights and protection.

It takes courage to navigate this system. It takes patience to understand its intricacies. But above all, it takes faith to believe that these laws, which can sometimes seem hostile, are there to provide a framework, stability, and that they are the expression of common human values: freedom, equality, justice.

For the immigrant, learning the laws of his new country also means accepting to change and adapt. It's a process that can be painful, because it reminds us that we are no longer in the comfort of our own landmarks, but in a new world that imposes its own rules. But it's a necessary step toward integration. By familiarizing themselves with these laws, immigrants learn to better understand and interact with the host society and earn respect in return.

But beyond the initial confrontation, there is also a promise hidden in these laws: that of possible inclusion, of equality to be achieved. For even if the road is long and full of pitfalls, each law carries with it the hope of recognition, of a full place in this new society. And it is by respecting these laws, by making them his or her own, that the immigrant can gradually transform this foreign land into a home.

In this way, laws become more than a set of rules to be followed. They become the bridge from exile to belonging. They are the means by which immigrants can claim their dignity, make their voices heard, and contribute to the society in which they seek to take root.

For an immigrant, these laws can sometimes seem incomprehensible or unfair because they are so different from those of his or her country of origin. For example, in some countries, homosexual relationships are punishable by law, while in the United States they are protected by the Constitution. In other countries, possession of certain substances, even in small amounts, can result in severe prison sentences, while in the United States these same substances are legal or decriminalized in some states.

The complexity of the American legal system, with its multiple layers of laws - federal, state, and local - adds to this confusion. For an immigrant, understanding these laws is crucial because violating them, even unintentionally, can have serious consequences, such as deportation or the inability to obtain citizenship. As a result, many immigrants live in fear of making a mistake, saying or doing something that could jeopardize their legal status or safety.

Social norms: what to say and what not to say

Beyond written laws, every society has its own social norms, unwritten rules that govern appropriate behavior in public and private. These norms are often subtle and unspoken, but failure to respect them can lead to social isolation, mistrust, and even hostility.

For an immigrant, these seemingly mundane social norms can become sources of profound misunderstanding and intense frustration. Imagine arriving in a new country and trying to adapt to customs you don't understand, where every gesture and word can be interpreted differently. In some cultures, refusing a gift or invitation is a sign of contempt, an unthinkable act. But in the United States, it's perfectly normal to politely decline an invitation without feeling uncomfortable. This difference, however subtle, can lead to uncomfortable situations for the person who wants to do the right thing but feels misunderstood.

Take time, for example. In many countries, the concept of punctuality is more flexible, and being a few minutes late, or even more, is not much of a reproach. But in American society, where punctuality is almost a sacred rule, being late can be perceived as a lack of seriousness or even a sign of disrespect. For the immigrant, adapting to this strictness requires not only changing habits, but also learning to decipher implicit expectations - those that are never actually said, but are deeply rooted in daily life.

These adjustments may seem small, but they go to the heart of each person's identity. They are a constant reminder to the immigrant that he or she is a stranger in this new environment, that he or she must make an effort to follow rules that still elude him or her. This is where the frustration comes in: the frustration of wanting to do the right thing, only to encounter repeated misunderstanding; the frustration of having to change to fit in and feeling like you're losing a part of yourself in the process.

But beyond the frustration, there's an immense lesson in humility and openness. By understanding and learning to respect these new norms, the immigrant forges a new identity enriched by this dual-cultural experience. He discovers that each society has its own codes and that, with time and patience, it's possible to navigate between these worlds without losing oneself.

It's in these small, everyday gestures, these invisible adjustments, that the complexity of integration lies. And that's where the beauty of immigration lies in the ability of each individual to embrace change, to find his or her place in an environment that is foreign at first, but eventually becomes familiar. Ultimately, beyond misunderstandings and frustrations, immigration is an act of hope, a bet on the future, and a fierce determination to build a better life in a world where every norm and every custom becomes an open door to integration and recognition.

These differences in perception and behavior create uncomfortable situations in which the immigrant may feel judged or misunderstood. They must learn to decode these norms, adapt to a new nonverbal language, and navigate a world of social conventions that are foreign to them.

Value Systems: Individualism vs. Collectivism

One of the most profound cultural shocks that immigrants experience when they arrive in the United States is related to the differences in fundamental values between their culture of origin and American culture. One of these major differences is the relationship between the individual and society.

In the United States, society is built on the fundamental pillars of individualism, personal autonomy, and the pursuit of individual happiness. These values are pervasive and shape every aspect of life, from education and family to work and leisure. Here, children are taught from an early age that they are the masters of their own destinies, and that it's up to them to chart their own course and define their own goals. Independence is exalted, and success, perceived as the fruit of individual effort, is an ideal to be pursued by all.

However, for an immigrant from a more communitarian culture, where solidarity and mutual aid are central, this emphasis on individualism can be challenging, disconcerting, and even destabilizing. In these societies, the family, the group, and the community are the foundations on which identity rests. Everyone draws strength and comfort from them, and individual success is often seen as a collective achievement. But in the United States, the weight of personal responsibility is immense. Each individual is expected to make his or her own decisions, chart his or her own course, and take full responsibility for both successes and failures.

For an immigrant, this can be a daunting reality. How do you find your place in a society that values autonomy above all else, where helping others can sometimes take a back seat? The pressure to succeed on your own, without the constant support of a close community, can be overwhelming. But it's also a tremendous opportunity: the chance to reinvent yourself, to prove that you can overcome obstacles, to chart your own course in a world where anything seems possible.

Far from isolation, American individualism is also a call to emancipation. It's an invitation to believe in yourself, to dream big, and to break free from the constraints of circumstance. Yes, the road is littered with pitfalls, and yes, the path to success can be lonely. But for those who accept the challenge, the United States offers the promise that with determination and courage, you can become the master of your own destiny.

For every immigrant who has left his or her homeland in the hope of a better life, this quest for individualism is an opportunity, a door to a future yet to be built, where dreams, no matter how big, can become reality. That is the power and beauty of the American experience.

In many other cultures, the collective takes precedence over the individual. Family, community, and interpersonal relationships play a central role in daily life. Important decisions are not made individually but in consultation with the family or group. The honor and reputation of the group are more important than personal desires.

Immigrants from these cultures may find it difficult to adjust to American individualistic values. They must learn to value their autonomy, express their opinions, take initiative, and accept competition. This transition is often painful because it challenges the self-image and deeply held values that have shaped their identity.

B. – An Immigrant's First Impressions of American Society: Expectations and Reality

When we decide to move to another country, especially one as iconic as the United States, we often bring with us dreams and expectations. The "American Dream," with its promise of freedom, prosperity, and success for all, continues to fascinate millions of people around the world. However, the reality of immigration is often very different from the images conveyed by the media and popular narratives.

Expectations: The American Dream

For many, the United States represents a country where anything is possible. We expect to find economic opportunity, social justice, and a better life for our children. The idea that through hard work and perseverance one can rise in society and achieve one's dreams is deeply ingrained in the minds of many immigrants.

The United States is perceived as a land of plenty, a country where human rights and individual freedoms are respected, a promised land. We expect to find an open, tolerant society that celebrates cultural diversity. Many dreams of building a home, starting a business, seeing their children graduate from the best universities. These expectations are fueled by the stories of those who left before them, by Hollywood movies, by the stories of celebrities who have succeeded against all odds.

The reality: between disillusionment and assimilation

Arriving in the United States is often a rude shock. First impressions are marked by the country's apparent grandeur and wealth: the skyscrapers of New York, the avenues of Los Angeles, and the gigantic shopping malls. But behind this facade, the reality is often more complex.

The economic reality is one of the first shocks. Finding a job is much harder than expected, especially if you don't speak English well or don't have the necessary skills. Many immigrants find themselves in precarious, low-wage, physically demanding jobs. For those who were professionals in their home country, this situation is particularly humiliating. They have to accept going back down the social ladder, to start from scratch, sometimes in very difficult working conditions.

The social reality is also disconcerting. Despite its diversity, American society is marked by profound inequalities, racial tensions, and a certain rejection of immigrants. Linguistic, cultural, and administrative barriers make integration difficult. Loneliness, isolation, and homesickness weigh heavily on the morale of newcomers. They often find themselves confined to ethnic communities, cut off from the rest of society, and feeling marginalized.

For many, the reality of immigration to the United States is a mixture of hope and disillusionment. They discover a country that is both fascinating and confusing, generous and ruthless, welcoming and suspicious. This complex reality requires a great capacity for adaptation, a constant effort to find one's place and build a new identity.

C. – Practical barriers: language, employment, housing and integration

Beyond the cultural and emotional aspects, immigration involves overcoming a series of practical obstacles that often determine the success or failure of the migration project. These daily challenges are many and varied, and their impact on immigrants' lives is considerable.

Language: a pervasive barrier

Language proficiency is perhaps the greatest challenge immigrants face. Without a good level of English, it is extremely difficult to find a decent job, navigate the administrative and healthcare systems, or even make social connections. The language barrier creates a sense of isolation and powerlessness by limiting opportunities for interaction and understanding.

For many, learning English is a daunting task. The cost of tuition, work-related fatigue, and family responsibilities make it a difficult undertaking. Children, on the other hand, adapt more quickly, often creating a generation gap. Parents then depend on their children to communicate with the outside world, which can lead to a loss of power and authority within the family.

Language is more than a tool for communication: it's a marker of identity. For immigrants, the need to speak English in order to succeed is a source of tension, as it can be perceived as an obligation to abandon part of their original culture. It's a constant dilemma between integration and preserving one's roots.

Employment: the key to economic independence

Finding a job is essential for any immigrant, as it is the key to economic independence and social integration. However, the American job market is difficult to access for those without the right qualifications, a network of contacts, or recognized experience.

Many immigrants find themselves in precarious, low-wage jobs far below their skills. They work in cleaning services, catering, construction or as domestic help. These jobs, which are often physically demanding, leave little time or energy to learn English or take training courses. For those who were doctors, engineers, or teachers in their home countries, this situation is particularly discouraging.

Obtaining diplomas or certifications recognized in the United States is often necessary to gain access to skilled jobs. But these courses are expensive and time-consuming. What's more, immigrants must juggle immediate financial needs, making the transition even more difficult.

Housing: the challenge of insecurity and discrimination

Finding adequate housing is one of the first challenges immigrants face when they arrive in the United States. This process is often fraught with financial, administrative, and sometimes even discriminatory barriers. Housing is much more than a roof over one's head: it is the foundation for stability and social integration.

For many immigrants, housing options are limited by their economic situation. The cost of living is exorbitant, especially in large cities where most employment opportunities are located. Renting an apartment or buying a house often requires a solid credit history, financial guarantees, or regularized immigration status. These requirements are difficult to meet for newcomers who have not had time to establish their financial or administrative situation.

Many immigrants then turn to neighborhoods where rents are more affordable, often in areas of high ethnic concentration. While these neighborhoods provide valuable community support, they are often associated with precarious living conditions: overcrowded, unsanitary, or poorly maintained housing. Access to basic services such as quality schools, public transportation, and health care is also limited.

Housing discrimination is a reality for many immigrants. Some landlords refuse to rent to people perceived as foreign or without legal status. This discrimination, sometimes subtle, creates a climate of mistrust and additional stress for families trying to build a stable home. The dream of a comfortable home becomes a never-ending quest punctuated by disappointment and sacrifice.

In the US, too, where a family life has a strong influence on the future of its children, not least through access to schools. This is because public schools are generally "funded by local property taxes," meaning that wealthier neighborhoods with more expensive real estate receive more funding for their schools. These additional resources allow for better infrastructure, more qualified teachers, and enriched educational programs.

As a result, children living in more affluent neighborhoods benefit from access to higher quality schools, often rated "A" or "B" on national assessments, with a wide range of educational resources. On the other hand, schools in less affluent neighborhoods receive less funding, which often affects the quality of education, with fewer educational materials, overworked teachers, and aging infrastructure.

This disparity in school quality has a direct impact on children's futures, as better primary and secondary education often paves the way to prestigious universities and greater career opportunities. Children from disadvantaged neighborhoods, on the other hand, are more likely to be educated in underperforming schools, which can limit their future prospects, particularly in terms of access to higher education and personal development.

In addition, residential and school segregation often reflect racial and economic inequalities, perpetuating cycles of social injustice in which children from poor, often minority, families do not have the same educational opportunities as those from more affluent families. Where one lives in the U.S. plays a critical role in the quality of education children receive, which in the long run affects their career opportunities and futures.

Integration: a journey fraught with pitfalls

Integration is one of the most complex aspects of the migration process. It's not only about adapting to a new environment but also about feeling accepted and respected in this new space. For immigrants, this integration goes through many stages, from learning the language to actively participating in community life.

The barriers to integration are many. In addition to language and economic difficulties, immigrants often face negative stereotypes and prejudices. They are sometimes perceived as intruders, competitors for jobs, or burdens on welfare systems. These perceptions, fueled by political and media discourse, create a climate of hostility that makes integration even more difficult.

One of the major challenges is to strike a balance between adapting to the culture of the host country and preserving one's own cultural identity. Many immigrants face contradictory pressures: they are asked to integrate but also to give up part of their cultural heritage in order to conform to local norms.

This tension is particularly acute for young people, who must navigate between the expectations of their parents and those of American society.

Integration programs, where they exist, do not always meet the real needs of immigrants. Access to quality English classes, appropriate job training, or mental health services is often limited by funding or political constraints. As a result, many immigrants are left to fend for themselves as they try to navigate a complex and often hostile system.

Integration isn't just about learning English or understanding the codes of this complex society. It's about learning to be an American while keeping what you are, what you've always been. And time is money in this country. In fact, the time it takes to assimilate is not measured in months or years. It's measured in steps taken, in connections made, in victories over obstacles, no matter how small. It's the moment when you no longer feel like an outsider, the moment when you feel accepted, and most importantly, when you accept yourself in this new context. It's the day when the immigrant stops feeling like an outsider. It's a long process for some, but it can take a long time. It can take a long time for some.

I truly believe that integration is a quest for dignity, an assertion of one's right to exist in a space that did not see us born, but that ends up welcoming us. It's a silent but essential conquest. An immigrant fights every day to prove that he belongs to this country, that he is a vital force in it. And the day he finally feels that his voice counts, that his contributions are recognized, he knows that he has become an inseparable part of the American fabric.

A journey of resilience and transformation

Despite all these obstacles, the immigrant experience is also a journey of resilience, transformation, and triumph. Every challenge overcome, every barrier broken, every small step toward integration is a victory - not only for the individual, but for an entire community that dreams of a better future. Immigrants, especially Haitians, bring a priceless treasure: their skills, their unique perspectives, their rich and deep culture. They enrich American society, bringing the vitality that only diversity can provide.

Crossing borders and weathering the storms of exile, these Haitians have left an indelible mark on the history of the United States. They turned adversity into opportunity, and their names resonate today as symbols of success, inspiration, and pride.

Consider Jean Baptiste Point du Sable, the pioneer who founded the city of Chicago. Born in Haiti, he laid the foundation for a city that would become one of America's greatest metropolises. Point du Sable embodies the strength of Haitian entrepreneurship and the visionary spirit that guides so many of our compatriots, such as Jeff Lozama, an entrepreneur who forged a destiny in the face of adversity and overcame all odds.

Others, like Edwidge Danticat, have used the power of their words to tell our stories. Their stories not only gave voice to the voiceless, but also introduced the world to the beauty, complexity, and resilience of the Haitian people.

Wyclef Jean, global music icon. His career, which began with The Fugees, is a symbol of Haitians' ability to excel in the arts while remaining true to their roots.

Pierre Antoine Garçon Former NFL player, Pierre A. Garçon excelled on American football fields, honoring his Haitian heritage while becoming a role model for young Haitians passionate about the sport.

The current Illinois Attorney General, Mr. Kwame Raoul, was appointed Illinois State Senator for the 13th District in November 2004, replacing Barack Obama, who was elected to the U.S. Senate and will become President of the United States in 2008.

The DesRoches brothers, Pascal, who became CFO of one of the largest cellular phone companies in the U.S., AT&T. Reginald, who presides over one of the largest private research universities in the U.S., RICE UNIVERSITY. And not only him, a black woman, the daughter of a Haitian immigrant, rose to the top at Harvard and became president of the world's leading university.

Add to this short list one of Hollywood's best black actresses, Garcelle Beauvais, Jimmy Jean Louis, Samuel Dalembert, Jerry H. Duplesis, Skal Labissiere, Marleine Bastien, Frandley Denis Julien, Wilkenson Sejour, Pasteur Gregory Toussaint, Dr. Henri Ronald Ford, Guy Webern Guerrier, Johnson Napoleon, James Pierre; The Dumorné brothers, who created one of the most classic clothing lines; Jean Michel Phillias and Rodney Noel, who created the largest Haitian music event in Miami. Karine Jean-Pierre, who rose to the top of the American political elite by becoming the first black female White House Press Secretary under the Biden administration.

Not to mention the descendants of immigrants: Jean Michel Basquiat, whose father fled the Duvalier dictatorship; Jarell "Big Baby" Miller, one of the great boxers of his generation; Sheila McCormick Sherfilus, who grew up here in the U.S. with the rigidity of Haitian parents and became a congresswoman; Mia Love, the first black Republican woman in Congress, as well as the first woman of Haitian descent to be elected to the U.S. Congress. And let's not forget the thousands of Haitian doctors, engineers, artists and social workers who, far from the spotlight, are building a stronger, more humane America every day. They bring their know-how, their courage, and their unwavering faith in a better future.

These names are just a few of many. They remind us that despite hardships, Haitians have made their mark and paved their way to success in the United States. Their journey is a source of inspiration for every immigrant who leaves his or her homeland not just to survive, but to triumph. They show us that even in the face of obstacles, hope, resilience, and faith in oneself can transform the dream of exile into a reality of success and dignity.

Arriving in a new country is an ordeal that tests the limits of human resilience. Immigrants must navigate between their dreams of a better life and the often-harsh realities of everyday life. They face practical, emotional, and social obstacles that sometimes seem insurmountable. Yet every immigration story is also one of transformation, self-discovery, and reinvention.

By overcoming the challenges of language, employment, housing, and integration, immigrants help shape American society. Their journeys are a testament to the strength of the human spirit and the ability of people to reinvent themselves in the face of adversity. They remind us that behind every face is a story of courage, sacrifice, and hope.

It's clear that the contribution of Haitians in the United States is an integral part of the country's social and economic fabric. Their presence has shaped various aspects of American life, from business and culture to education and community service. By developing this reflection with concrete data, we can better appreciate the significant impact of this community on the American landscape.

A Statistical Overview of the Haitian Diaspora

According to the U.S. Census Bureau, the Haitian diaspora in the United States is estimated at approximately 1.2 million people. This population is primarily concentrated in Florida, in the Miami and Fort Lauderdale areas, as well as in New York, Boston, and other major U.S. cities.

d. – Economic Contribution

According to the 2021 American Community Survey (ACS) report, Haitian immigrants have a high rate of participation in various sectors of the economy. Nearly 30% of Haitians are employed in service occupations, including health care and social assistance, reflecting a strong presence in essential and often low-wage jobs that are critical to the day-to-day functioning of society.

Haitian entrepreneurs also play an important role. According to a study by the Kauffman Foundation, approximately 11% of Haitian entrepreneurs in the United States own small businesses. These businesses range from restaurants and shops to hair salons and travel agencies. These businesses are not only a source of income for their owners but also create jobs for members of the community and for Americans in the surrounding area.

e. – Impact on the Education System

Many Haitians work as teachers, school counselors, and administrators. According to a study by the Institute for Immigration Research, about 20% of Haitian immigrants have college degrees and a significant percentage work in education. They play a critical role in supporting students from diverse communities and help enrich educational programs with unique and diverse perspectives.

Local academic institutions also benefit from the presence of Haitian students. Haitian students are often recognized for their hard work and resilience, and many receive scholarships for academic excellence. The impact of their academic success is felt not only within their institutions, but also in the community, where they inspire younger generations to pursue higher education and professional careers.

f. – Cultural Contribution

Culturally, Haitians bring an invaluable wealth to American society. Their culture, deeply rooted in a rich and varied history, is reflected in many aspects of American life. Haitian festivals, such as the Miami Carnival, have become major events that attract participants from all backgrounds, promoting greater cross-cultural understanding and enriching the American cultural scene.

Haitian cuisine is another example of this cultural contribution. Haitian restaurants, such as those specializing in "griot," "diri ak pwa," and other traditional dishes, have grown in popularity and contribute to the culinary diversity of the United States. These restaurants not only serve food, but also provide spaces for Haitian Americans and other communities to meet and share culture.

g. – Social and Community Impact

Haitian immigrants also play a significant role in supporting their communities and in community development efforts. Many Haitian community organizations provide essential services such as legal services, translation services, and support programs for newcomers. Organizations such as Family Action Network Movement

(FANM), Florida Immigration Coalition (FLIC); Love By Action in Charity (LAC) work to improve the lives of Haitians in the United States by providing resources and support to families and individuals.

Haitian contributions to these organizations strengthen the local social fabric and help create important support networks. They play a leading role in humanitarian and relief efforts, particularly in response to natural disasters in Haiti, by organizing fundraising events and providing material and financial assistance to those affected by these crises.

CHAPTER FOUR

CONSCIENCE OF POLITICAL ISSUES

I was attracted to American political life long before I came to live here. I studied it at Science Po, and I've always admired the democracy they've built over time. When I was very young, I was 12 at the time, I fell under the spell of Bill Clinton. Not only did he bring President Aristide back to Haiti, he had his honeymoon in Haiti with Hillary in 1975, but above all, in my humble opinion, he was in the line of great statesmen like Jacques Chirac, who was my role model thanks to the various French magazines that Maman subscribed to. A politician must above all be a speaker, able to promote his ideas. I could see him speaking in English as if he were speaking in French, his voice, the musicality. He's the first American to be added to my list of generally French political role models. I do not regret having admired him, but great admiration often leads to great disappointment. When he restored democracy in Haiti in 1994, it wasn't so that we could make the democratic transition we needed before the turn of the millennium, but rather so that he could become the American czar of the Republic of Haiti, the man who could change America and change the destiny of relations between Haiti and the United States. Because we failed to make the democratic transition, we became a failed state, so many of us think that our future lies elsewhere, in the United States.

How do you put all your eggs in the American basket when American democracy is learning to be less and less moral? Who learns to lay siege to the Capitol? When immigration becomes the only reason, some people get into politics and want to become president of the world's leading power?

h. – Immigration in American Political Discourse: An Analysis of Recent Immigration Policy

Immigration has always been a hot topic in American political discourse. Since the founding of the United States, the question of who has the right to settle here and under what conditions has been a source of conflict and compromise. From the passage of the Chinese Exclusion Act in 1882 to the Immigration Act of 1965, which redefined the quota system, each historical period has set its own rules for the reception and integration of newcomers.

In recent decades, the polarization around the issue of migration has steadily increased. Immigration has become an ideological marker and a central issue in electoral campaigns, exacerbating divisions between different political currents. On the one hand, some see immigrants as a threat to jobs, security, and national identity. On the other hand, many see immigration as a vital force for demographic renewal, innovation and cultural diversity.

Recent immigration policy, particularly under the Obama, Trump, and Biden administrations, illustrates this polarization. The Obama administration, despite its stated desire to reform the immigration system, disappointed some of its supporters with record levels of deportations while attempting to establish protections for certain immigrant groups, such as the Dreamers. The Trump administration, on the other hand, has radicalized the discourse on immigration by implementing zero-tolerance policies, building a wall on the southern border, and imposing travel bans on certain predominantly Muslim countries. These policies, often accompanied by stigmatizing language, have reinforced the image of immigrants as "invaders.

Under the Biden administration, the migration issue has taken a new turn. The president has reversed some of his predecessor's most controversial policies, such as the travel ban and family separation, while attempting to promote comprehensive reform of the immigration system. However, the surge in arrivals at the southern border and the management of asylum seekers pose significant challenges. Often criticized by the right for being too lax and by the left for not being progressive enough, Biden's policy demonstrates the difficulty of finding consensus on this complex issue.

The evolution of the political discourse around immigration has also been marked by a rise in populism, where the issue of migration is often instrumentalized to stoke fears and win votes. Anti-immigrant populism feeds on a rhetoric of crisis and existential threat, presenting immigrants as scapegoats for economic and social problems. This dynamic, far from being unique to the United States, reflects a global trend in which anxieties associated with globalization and the rapid transformation of societies are channeled into opposition to immigration.

In this context, it is crucial to understand that the issue of immigration cannot be reduced to numbers or flows of people. It goes to the heart of the values and principles on which American democracy is based. How do we reconcile openness, diversity, and integration with the imperatives of security, order, and social cohesion? This is the complex question facing policymakers and society as a whole.

i. – How Immigration Redefines Notions of Freedom, Equality, and Inclusion in American Society

Immigration doesn't just bring new people to American soil; it challenges the very foundations of society by redefining notions of freedom, equality, and inclusion. These principles, at the heart of the American project, are being tested by the realities of the migration phenomenon.

Freedom: For many, America is first and foremost a land of freedom. This idea is rooted in the country's history, based on the rejection of tyranny and the search for a space where everyone can aspire to a better life. Immigrants fleeing persecution, poverty, or lack of opportunity in their home countries embody this quest for freedom. But this long-awaited freedom often encounters bureaucratic and social barriers once they set foot on American soil.

Access to freedom is also unequally distributed. Some immigrants, such as refugees or asylees, come seeking protection from imminent danger. But the process of obtaining legal status is often long and uncertain, leaving thousands of people in a precarious situation. As for the undocumented, they live in the shadows, under constant threat of deportation and deprived of many basic rights.

Equality: The principle of equality is a central pillar of American democracy. Yet immigration reveals profound inequalities in the way individuals are treated. Depending on their origin, legal status, or even occupation, immigrants do not have the same opportunities for integration and success. Skilled immigrants can obtain work visas, while those who arrive with few resources are often relegated to precarious, low-wage jobs.

Discrimination at both institutional and societal levels undermines the principle of equality. Racial and ethnic prejudice, stereotypes of "good" and "bad" immigrants, and inequalities in access to education and health care illustrate how discrimination undermines the principle of equality. Equality is far from being achieved. Equality of opportunity, promised to all, sometimes seems unattainable for those from abroad.

Inclusion: Inclusion is the idea that everyone, regardless of background, can participate fully in the life of the community. Immigration enriches American society by bringing new cultures, languages, and perspectives. But it also poses challenges to integration and social cohesion. How do we create a society where differences are valued rather than perceived as threats?

Debates about inclusion often focus on symbolic issues: the right to wear religious symbols in public, the use of languages other than English, or the representation of minorities in the media. But real inclusion requires concrete policies: access to quality education, the fight against discrimination in the labor market, the recognition of foreign diplomas, etc. Inclusion isn't just about tolerating differences; it's about creating a space where everyone can thrive and contribute.

Immigration profoundly redefines the notions of freedom, equality, and inclusion. It reminds us that these principles are not given, but ideals to which we must constantly strive. It also demonstrates that American democracy is an evolving project that must reinvent itself to meet the challenges of each era.

j. – The Racial Dimension

The issue of immigration to the United States cannot be fully understood without acknowledging the racial dimension that underlies it. For centuries, U.S. immigration policy has been marked by racial biases that have favored certain groups while marginalizing others. Black immigrants, particularly Haitians, face systematic discrimination that reflects a broader history of racism deeply rooted in American society. In the '80s, a certain America preferred Cubans to Haitians; today, it's Ukrainians.

For black immigrants, integration in the United States is often a double struggle. They face not only the usual challenges of immigration - language, employment, legal status - but also the brutal reality of racism. This discrimination manifests itself in many ways: higher rates of asylum denials for Haitians, inhumane detention conditions at the border, and mass deportations that demonstrate unequal treatment compared to other immigrant groups.

Immigration isn't just about politics or economics; it's also about racial justice. The statistics are clear: Black immigrants, especially those from Haiti, are more likely to be arrested, detained and deported than white immigrants.

This reality reflects an implicit hierarchy of lives in which some are deemed more worthy of protection than others.

The issue of race in immigration exposes an American paradox: a country that prides itself on being a land of opportunity, but often denies that opportunity to those whose skin color does not conform to an implicit norm. While the United States prides itself on being a country of diversity and inclusion, immigration policies continue to reinforce systems of segregation and marginalization.

It's impossible to talk about immigration without talking about race. Discussions about "waves" of immigration are often colored by racial stereotypes, irrational fears, and political discourses that demonize certain immigrant groups. This is particularly true of blacks, who have historically been perceived as a threat rather than an asset.

Haitians, who fought for their independence in 1804, embody this ongoing quest for freedom and dignity. Yet centuries later, they face an America that is still reluctant to offer them that dignity. The racial dimension of immigration forces us to ask difficult questions: Why are some immigrants welcomed with open arms while others are turned away or criminalized? Why does black skin remain a stigmatizing factor in a country that holds itself up as a model of democracy?

Racial justice cannot be separated from migration justice. To move forward, the United States must recognize that its migration system is broken not only by outdated laws, but also by the racial biases that inform those laws. Only by acknowledging this reality can we hope to build a more just system, one in which every life, regardless of color, is treated with respect, dignity, and humanity.

Haitians, like so many other black immigrants, are asking for one thing: the opportunity to live and contribute in a country that claims to be a beacon of freedom. It's time for America to live up to that promise, for everyone, regardless of race.

k. – The Issue of Integration and Immigrant Rights Debates

The integration of immigrants into American society is a complex process influenced by economic, social, and political factors. One of the most heated debates concerns access to citizenship and the civil and social rights of immigrants. These issues touch directly on the definition of political community: who is included in the "we" of the American nation?

Access to Citizenship: American citizenship is more than a legal status; it is an expression of commitment to the country and a recognition of belonging to the national community. For many immigrants, becoming a citizen is an achievement, a sign of success and integration. But the road to naturalization is fraught with pitfalls. Application processing times, continuous residency requirements, language and cultural tests, and high costs discourage many potential candidates.

The debate over access to citizenship also focuses on the fate of the millions of undocumented immigrants living in the United States. Should they be offered a path to legalization, or should repression and deportation be stepped up? Proponents of legalization point to the economic and social contributions of these invisible workers, while opponents insist on respect for the law and national sovereignty.

Civil and social rights: Even without citizenship, immigrants should enjoy certain basic rights. In practice, however, these rights are often violated. Undocumented migrants, for example, live in extreme precariousness, deprived of basic rights such as access to health care, higher education, or protection from abuse in the workplace. Fear of deportation often prevents them from claiming their rights or denouncing situations of exploitation.

Debates on the social rights of immigrants have intensified with the restrictive policies implemented in recent years. Access to social services, public health care, and education for the children of immigrants has been called into question by local and national legislation. These restrictions, often justified on budgetary or security grounds, make already vulnerable populations even more vulnerable.

Economic and social integration: Integration is not only about acquiring rights, but also about being able to participate fully in the economic and social life of the country. This means access to decent employment, quality education and health services, and recognition of skills and qualifications acquired abroad. The barriers to this integration are many: discrimination in the labor market, difficulties in getting qualifications recognized, lack of networks and support.

Today, the evidence is clear: immigration is a major challenge to American democracy. It challenges the founding principles of freedom, equality, and inclusion, and forces society to confront its contradictions and prejudices. Recent immigration policies demonstrate the difficulty of balancing the imperatives of security, justice, and humanity.

The integration of immigrants, with all its difficulties, is a test for American democracy. How can we include these newcomers in the common project? How can we guarantee their rights while respecting the laws and institutions of the country? Far from being abstract, these questions have concrete implications for millions of people.

To meet this challenge, we must go beyond simplistic rhetoric and recognize the complexity of the migration issue. We need to build a society where everyone, regardless of their background, can find their place and contribute to our collective prosperity. Far from being a threat, immigration is an opportunity to renew and enrich the American democratic project.

Democratic and Republican Party Positions on Immigration: A Comparative Analysis

It's one of the most controversial and debated issues in American politics. The positions of the two major U.S. political parties, the Democratic Party and the Republican Party, differ profoundly on this issue, reflecting different political philosophies and priorities. This comparative analysis explores these divergences and highlights the implications for immigration policy and American values.

A. – Democratic Party Positions

The Democratic Party generally takes a more liberal approach to immigration, advocating more inclusive and humanitarian policies. Here are the main aspects of their position:

— Comprehensive Immigration Reform: Democrats support comprehensive reform of the immigration system to legalize the status of undocumented immigrants. They support a path to citizenship for immigrants who have been in the country for a long time and have contributed positively to society. The Dream Act, for example, is Democratic-sponsored legislation that would provide a path to citizenship for young immigrants brought to the country illegally as children.

— Protect refugees and asylum seekers: The Democratic Party supports more generous asylum policies and stronger protections for refugees. They support fair asylum processes and the protection of asylum seekers' rights and emphasize humanity and compassion in the treatment of people fleeing persecution.

— Defending immigrant rights: Democrats support the civil and human rights of immigrants, including access to health care, education, and labor rights. They seek to protect immigrants from discrimination and abuse and to ensure that immigration laws are not unfairly or discriminatorily applied.

– Reduce restrictions: The Democratic Party generally supports reducing visa restrictions and expanding opportunities for skilled and unskilled workers. They believe that immigrants make an essential contribution to the American economy and support policies that promote their integration.

B. – Republican Party Positions

In marked contrast to their Democratic counterparts, the Republican Party takes a more restrictive, security-oriented approach to immigration:

– Strengthening Border Security: Republicans place a strong emphasis on border security and combating illegal immigration. They advocate measures such as building walls or physical barriers along the southern border, as well as increased funding for border security and strict enforcement of immigration laws.

– Reducing routes of entry: The Republican Party often favors reducing the number of visas issued and the avenues for legal immigration. They advocate tighter restrictions on visa programs, including work and family visas, to limit immigration.

– Deportation and Enforcement: Republicans support a more aggressive deportation policy and strict enforcement of immigration laws. They advocate the deportation of illegal immigrants and seek to prohibit the use of social services and public benefits by undocumented people.

– Immigration Reform: While some Republicans support specific immigration reforms, such as changing visa programs for skilled workers, their proposals tend to include more restrictive measures and stricter conditions for legalizing immigrants.

C. – Implications for Migration Policy

The divergent positions of the two parties have important implications for U.S. migration policy:

For Democrats: The Democrats' emphasis on inclusiveness and comprehensive reform aims to create a more humane and just immigration system. Their approach could foster better integration of immigrants and promote values of compassion and diversity. However, implementation of these policies could face political obstacles, particularly due to disagreements with Republicans and legislative challenges.

- For Republicans: The Republican focus on border security and immigration restriction is designed to address concerns about illegal immigration and national security. Their approach could strengthen border control and limit immigration, but it could also create tensions with immigrant communities and affect perceptions of the U.S. as a welcoming place.

D. – Toward a consensus?

While the two parties' positions may seem diametrically opposed, there are areas where consensus could emerge. Issues such as visa reform for skilled workers, protection of immigrant rights, and border security are points of debate where compromise could be reached. Creating a balanced immigration policy that addresses both national security and immigrant rights could provide a path to constructive reform.

The positions of the Democratic and Republican parties on immigration reflect profoundly different visions of migration policy and American values. While Democrats emphasize inclusiveness and human rights, Republicans favor security and restriction. Understanding these positions is essential for assessing current and future U.S. immigration policy and for thinking about how to promote constructive dialogue and effective immigration reform. The challenge is to navigate these divergent perspectives to build an immigration system that reflects the core values of justice, security, and humanity.

CHAPTER FIVE

CONSCIENCE OF THE DOUBLE CONSCIOUSNESS

Even though many of them leave their country never to return and don't feel any more concerned about what is happening in their homeland, for us Haitians it is impossible. We can never leave Haiti. If we dare, a bird will remind us; that we can't leave Haiti. After the assassination of President Jovenel Moïse on the night of July 7-8, 2021, it took me some time to accept that it had really happened; I convinced myself that politics in Haiti was over for me. When the earthquake hit the south of the country in August, I couldn't resist calling a few friends to mobilize aid for my country, and we founded Do Better. As we all sat in front of our televisions one night and watched a ranger on a horse chasing a Haitian with a whip in his hand, the next day I mobilized friends and "GuyWewe Radio a" to go to the border to defend our compatriots, and so on. There was always a reason for Haiti to occupy our hearts and minds, so I became aware that I was an immigrant and a citizen at the same time.

a. – The Concept of "Double Consciousness": Straddling Two Worlds

The concept of "double consciousness," conceptualized by W.E.B. Du Bois in the early 20th century, describes the feeling of being constantly observed, judged by criteria that are not one's own, and having to navigate between two conflicting identities. Du Bois used this idea to explore the experience of African Americans torn between their black and American identities in a deeply racist society. However, the concept resonates particularly powerfully with the experience of immigrants to the U.S., who also find themselves juggling between their original cultural heritage and the expectations of the host country.

For an immigrant, "double consciousness" means living simultaneously with the gaze of the country of origin, often imbued with nostalgia and traditional values, and the gaze of the host society, which may be fraught with prejudice or misunderstanding. This creates a constant tension: How do you stay true to your roots while embracing the opportunities and values of the new world? How do you live up to the expectations of your home community while striving to integrate into a society that sometimes views you as an outsider?

This split consciousness creates a tug-of-war between the desire to preserve one's cultural identity and the need to adapt to a new environment. The immigrant is a tightrope walker, trying to maintain a precarious balance between two realities. On the one hand, they must honor the traditions, language, and values of their country of origin. On the other hand, they must adopt new habits, learn a new language, and understand different cultural codes. This situation can lead to a certain confusion of identity, and a sense of loss, but also to a unique inner richness. A Haitian is not an Afro-American, and vice versa; imagine the Haitian immigrant suffered the fate of blacks when this society was built; imagine if Afro-Americans also had the anti-immigrant attitude of America?

Reflections on double consciousness:

Dual consciousness is a complex challenge, but it's also an opportunity. Immigrants who navigate between their original cultural identities and their new lives in the United States bring a wealth of perspectives and skills. This dual identity enables them to play a unique role in American society, bridging different cultures and enriching the country's cultural, economic, and social landscape.

The process of reconciling one's own values with those of the host country is both a personal journey and a collective contribution. By seeking to reconcile these two aspects of their identity, immigrants actively participate in creating a more inclusive and understanding society. Their presence and commitment help redefine the notion of belonging. American identity, transforming it into a plural identity that embraces diversity as a strength.

Dual consciousness can also be a source of pride. It embodies the ability of immigrants to turn challenges into opportunities, to navigate between two worlds, and to create a space where their values and aspirations can coexist. This dual consciousness enriches not only the lives of immigrants themselves, but also American society as a whole, contributing to a culture of dialogue, understanding, and mutual respect.

b. – Reconciling the values of home and host countries

One of the greatest challenges immigrants face is reconciling the values of their country of origin with those of the host country. This reconciliation is not merely an act of adaptation, but a genuine reconfiguration of identity. Values, whether cultural, religious or social, shape our vision of the world and influence our choices. For immigrants, this process of reconciliation can sometimes seem like a compromise, even a betrayal of their origins. But it can also be an enrichment, a way of forging a new hybrid identity.

Family and community values: In many cultures of origin, family and community play a central role. Intergenerational relationships, respect for elders, and mutual aid within the community are fundamental pillars. In the United States, however, society values individualism, independence, and personal autonomy. This divergence in values can lead to conflict, especially within immigrant families, where children raised in the American context adopt behaviors and aspirations that are sometimes at odds with those of their parents. How, then, can the family unit be preserved while allowing each member to flourish in his or her own environment?

Integration should not mean abandoning one's original values. On the contrary, immigrants have the capacity to bring new perspectives and lifestyles that enrich the host society. Respect for family and community values can be combined with individual aspirations to create a model of integration in which each person's identity is respected and valued.

Religious values: Religion plays an essential role in the lives of many immigrants. It is often the last refuge, the source of comfort and identity in a foreign environment. However, religious practices can sometimes conflict with the norms and expectations of the host country. Wearing religious symbols, eating habits and specific holidays are all potential points of friction.

To reconcile these religious values with those of a secular and pluralistic American society, it is essential to promote dialogue and mutual understanding. The freedom of religion enshrined in the U.S. Constitution must allow everyone to practice their faith without fear of discrimination. But this freedom also requires respect for the country's fundamental laws and values, such as gender equality and freedom of expression. Striking a balance between respect for individual beliefs and adherence to democratic principles is a constant challenge, but one that is essential to a harmonious society.

Political and social values: Immigrants bring with them political and social views shaped by their experiences in their country of origin. These may sometimes conflict with the ideals and practices of the host country. For example, an immigrant from a country where women's rights are limited may experience culture shock as she discovers American society's expectations and norms regarding gender equality.

Reconciling these values requires education and open-mindedness. It's not simply a matter of assimilation but of exchange and mutual learning. Immigrants must not only learn to understand and respect the values of their host country, but they must also be willing to share and explain the values of their country of origin. It's in this exchange that true integration lies, the kind that creates a fairer, more inclusive society.

c. – The Contributions of immigrants to American society and the Perceptions of it

Immigrants play a critical role in the building and development of American society. Their contributions go far beyond traditional stereotypes that confine them to certain sectors of the economy or to subordinate roles. In fact, immigrants enrich American society in many ways - economically, culturally, socially, and politically.

Economic contributions: The idea that immigrants take jobs from Americans is one of the most pervasive and persistent myths. In reality, immigrants make significant contributions to the U.S. economy, whether by starting businesses, innovating, or working in critical sectors where native-born workers are in short supply. According to numerous studies, immigrants are more entrepreneurial than the native-born. They are starting businesses, creating jobs, and boosting the economy. Tech giants like Google, Tesla, and Apple were all founded or co-founded by immigrants or the children of immigrants.

Immigrant workers are also essential in sectors like agriculture, construction, and human services. They often fill jobs that native-born Americans are reluctant to take, contributing to the country's overall economic prosperity. Far from being a drain on the economy, immigrants are a valuable resource that stimulates growth and innovation.

Cultural contributions: American culture is by definition a melting pot, an amalgam of diverse influences that come together to create a unique identity.

Immigrants enrich this cultural mosaic with their traditions, languages, cuisines, music, and arts. They bring new ways of thinking, new aesthetics, and new flavors that eventually integrate and influence the dominant culture.

Many American artistic, literary, and musical movements have been influenced by waves of immigration. From jazz, born of African slave traditions and European influences, to fusion cuisines that combine ingredients and techniques from around the world, American culture is a living testimony to the contributions of immigrants.

Social and Political Contributions: Immigrants also bring new social and political perspectives. Their experience of injustices and challenges in their home countries can make them particularly sensitive to issues of civil rights and social justice. Many immigrants become involved in social movements, advocacy groups, or politics to defend the interests of their communities and promote a more just society. By actively participating in civic life, immigrants demonstrate that they are not simply passive recipients of the American Dream but committed actors in nation-building. Their involvement in the political process, whether at the local or national level, demonstrates their desire to contribute fully to the society that welcomes them.

The perception of immigrants: Despite their invaluable contributions, immigrants are often perceived ambivalently, even negatively, by a segment of the American population. Stereotypes and prejudices persist immigrants are said to be "too many," "taking jobs from Americans," "taking advantage of the system," or even "taking advantage of the world."

"These perceptions are often fueled by populist political rhetoric. These perceptions are often fueled by populist political rhetoric that instrumentalizes the migration issue to stir up fears and divide society. They forget the consequences because Trump has attacked us without any justification, students of Haitian origin are being intimidated in schools everywhere; today the Dominican Republic is deporting around 10,000 Haitians a week.

The negative perceptions often conveyed in the media and by some politicians can create an atmosphere of mistrust and division, not only in the United States but elsewhere. But it's important to remember that these perceptions do not reflect the full reality of the immigrant experience. Immigrants are human beings with dreams, aspirations, and a deep desire to make a positive contribution to their host society. Ultimately, they don't just want to survive, they want to thrive and contribute to the community.

The Contribution of Immigrants to American society:

The contributions of immigrants are vast and varied, and their impact is profound in many important areas of American society:

1. Education and research: Immigrants play a critical role in education and scientific research. Many international researchers, teachers, and students contribute to innovation and scientific progress in the United States. American universities are often home to vibrant international student populations that bring fresh ideas and unique perspectives. This diversity stimulates research, fosters intellectual exchange, and enriches academic debate.

2. In the arts and media: Immigrants enrich the American artistic landscape by bringing a variety of cultural influences. The diversity of cultural backgrounds is reflected in literature, film, music, and the visual arts. The work of immigrant artists, often inspired by their own experiences, offers an alternative vision of the world and explores universal themes from new perspectives. These artistic contributions not only provide a better understanding of multicultural realities but also create an enriching intercultural dialogue.

3. In politics and social justice: Immigrants are often active advocates for civil rights and social reform. Their involvement in political and community life contributes to the development of public policy and the promotion of human rights. They bring unique experiences that enrich debates about social justice, equality, and the distribution of resources. As agents of change, they are powerful voices for inclusion and equity.

4. In business and entrepreneurship: Immigrants are key drivers of the U.S. economy. Not only do they fill important positions in a variety of sectors, but they are also dynamic entrepreneurs who start businesses, create jobs, and spur innovation. By launching start-ups and developing businesses, they contribute to the economic growth and competitiveness of the United States on the world stage.

5. In local communities: At the local level, immigrants actively participate in community life by forming associations, volunteering, and supporting community development efforts. They play a crucial role in strengthening the social fabric by creating support networks, facilitating the integration of newcomers, and promoting social cohesion.

The dual consciousness of the immigrant at the crossroads of two cultures is a complex but essential reality. It reveals the challenges and opportunities of navigating between a rich cultural past and a promising future in a new country. Immigrants bring invaluable wealth to American society, enriching its cultural, economic, and social fabric. By reconciling the values of their country of origin with those of their host country, they contribute to a more diverse, inclusive, and just society.

Reflecting on double consciousness is therefore an invitation to recognize and value the contributions of immigrants while reflecting on ways to promote harmonious integration that respects multiple identities. By embracing the complexity of dual consciousness, American society can move toward a future in which diversity is celebrated as a unifying force rather than a source of division.

The efforts that are required in Practice

For many immigrants, the United States represents a dream, a promise of freedom and opportunity. But this dream is not without challenges and sacrifices. It takes more than courage to succeed in this new country. It takes strategies, vision, and above all, an unwavering will to adapt without denying who you are. Here's some advice for any immigrant looking to build a solid future in the U.S. today.

a. – Learn the language with determination

Language is the key that unlocks all doors. Mastering English is not just a formality, it's an indispensable tool for success. Whether it's finding a job, integrating socially, or navigating the complexities of government, English is the bridge that connects you to this society. Take lessons, practice every day, and dive into conversations even if you feel uncomfortable. The more you master the language, the more confidence and opportunities you'll gain.

b. – Build a solid network

Connections count in the United States. Whether it's finding a job, understanding local laws or overcoming difficulties, a support network is essential. Surround yourself with people who understand your background, share your goals, or have been through the same challenges. Community associations, religious groups, professional associations, or even your neighbors can be invaluable allies. The path to integration is less lonely when you walk with others.

c. – Understand and Respect the Law

U.S. laws are strict and can sometimes be confusing for immigrants. Take the time to understand your rights and responsibilities. Never underestimate the importance of having current documentation: your immigration status is an absolute priority. Never engage in illegal practices, no matter how tempting. Following the rules will protect you and pave the way for a safer future. If necessary, don't hesitate to consult an immigration lawyer.

d. – Invest in education and skills

Whether you arrive with a degree or no education at all, education remains a formidable weapon. In the U.S., opportunities often match your skills. If you can, go back to school, take online courses, or learn a trade that's in demand. A new skill can change your future. Many immigrants have started small and worked their way up thanks to their investment in learning. Education is a steppingstone to a better future.

e. – Never Lose Your Roots

When you move to the United States, don't forget where you came from. Your roots are your strength. Your culture, language, and traditions are the richness you bring to this country. Never let the pressure to assimilate erase what makes you unique. The United States is a country of diversity, and by preserving your roots, you'll contribute to its richness. You can assimilate and still be proud of who you are.

f. – Show your resilience

Integration is not an easy journey. You'll face challenges, moments of discouragement, maybe even discrimination. But remember, every trial is a lesson. The greatest successes often come out of the greatest difficulties. Be patient, persevere, and believe in yourself. You're not alone in this journey; countless immigrants have overcome the same obstacles before you. Their resilience is proof that success is possible.

g. – Build your credit wisely

In the United States, your credit history is critical. It will determine your access to many opportunities: buying a home, a car, even renting an apartment. As soon as you arrive, start building good credit. Use a credit card wisely, pay your bills on time, and make sure you don't accumulate unnecessary debt. Good credit will open many doors for you.

Keep abreast of political developments

Immigration laws in the United States are constantly changing. What's true today may change tomorrow. Stay informed about immigration policy, your rights, and ongoing reforms. Your future and that of your family may be affected by political decisions. Vigilance is essential.

h. – Be kind to yourself

Immigrating is an intense adventure. At times you may feel exhausted, disoriented, or even isolated. This is normal. Take care of your mental and physical well-being. Seek support when you need it. No one can do it alone. Taking care of yourself is an important step toward long-term success.

i. – Never give up hope

Hope is the driving force behind every immigrant. It's the hope of a better life that drove you to cross borders, leave your home, and face the unknown. Never lose sight of that hope. There will be difficult moments, but always remember why you came. Every step, every effort matters. America, in all its complexity, is still a land of opportunity. If you keep that hope alive, you'll find your way to success.

As an immigrant to the United States, you are already an example of courage and determination. Your story, your struggles, and your successes help shape this country. You belong here, and with perseverance, you'll build the future you deserve.

j. – Play the lottery and not be addicted

For some immigrants to the United States, playing the lottery on a regular basis can seem like a way out or a ray of hope on an often-rocky road. The idea of winning a substantial sum of money that could change the course of one's life and that of one's family can be terribly tempting. After all, in a country where the American dream is often presented as a promise of prosperity, the hope that the lottery represents could, for many, embody this dream of rapid, painless social advancement.

But it's important to ask whether playing the lottery is really good advice for an immigrant or anyone for that matter. The odds of winning are infinitesimally small. For a hard-working immigrant, sometimes in precarious conditions and with few resources, every dollar invested in the lottery could be better used elsewhere: whether for his or her children's education, building savings, or investing in personal projects.

While there are stories of people becoming millionaires overnight thanks to the lottery, these stories often overshadow the day-to-day reality. Gambling addiction can become a trap, and instead of building a stable future, playing the lottery regularly can distance a person from their real goals.

Ultimately, the real "win" for an immigrant to the U.S. may lie less in lottery luck than in hard work, education, and resilience - values that do not promise instant wealth but do offer tangible results in the long run.

CHAPTER SIX

CONSCIENCE OF THE CHALLENGES AND RICHNESS OF DIVERSITY

It was my late literature teacher, Joseph Jacques Florvil, who gave us the goal of being an intellectual, why we went to school, why we had to travel. It was for the sole purpose of being satisfied with being a citizen of the world. It was an absolute dream. The wealth of diversity that the United States has to offer will allow me to prove right this man who has shaped my whole life, and who I wanted to be like at all costs. By participating in all these events, I've become visible in the community, I'm starting to work in elections, I'm receiving awards, the city of North Miami Beach has even declared April 19th Alexandre Telfort Fils Day. It's as if America is opening its arms to me. Meanwhile, I take part in conferences and popular events with the participation of several nations. And that's where I'm going to break through the barriers of my community and really open up to other communities, thanks to what Haiti has offered me in terms of education. Even if I didn't speak English or Spanish or Italian properly, I chatted with every new face and made a good impression on university professors who opened doors for me, lawyers, entrepreneurs, religious people, students from all nations. I put myself to the test and these enriching experiences made me realize that I was a Haitian citizen of the world; and I loved my country even more. In the face of diversity, I understood that I had my place as a Haitian, and in less than 5 years, I would come from Italy as a simple immigrant to climb the same podium as Kamala Harris, the Vice President of the United States, as a black leader influencing the world.

a. – Immigration as a vector of cultural enrichment: the contribution of different waves of immigration to the construction of the United States

Immigration is a fundamental pillar of American history, and its role in the cultural enrichment of the country cannot be underestimated. Since its earliest days, the country has welcomed successive waves of immigrants who have helped shape American society as we know it today. Each immigrant group has brought a part of its cultural heritage, traditions, and skills, enriching the cultural, social, and economic fabric of the United States.

Waves of Immigration and their contributions

The first waves of immigration, which took place in the 17th and 18th centuries, saw the arrival of European settlers, primarily British, Dutch, German, and French. These early immigrants brought with them their languages, customs, and legal systems, helping to form the cultural and institutional foundations of the young American nation.

In the 19th century, the United States experienced a massive influx of immigrants, particularly from Ireland, Germany, Italy, and Scandinavia. These immigrants played a crucial role in the country's expansion and industrialization. The Irish worked on the railroads and in the mines, the Germans brought culinary traditions and craftsmanship, and the Italians enriched American culture with their artistic and culinary contributions. This mix of cultures created an increasingly diverse American society.

The 20th century was marked by waves of immigration from Latin America, Asia, and the Middle East. These immigrants brought new cultural, linguistic, and social dimensions. Chinese and Japanese communities, for example, played an important role in the development of infrastructure and the economy. Latin American immigrants have enriched American society with their music, cuisine, and vibrant culture. Immigrants from the Middle East have brought new religious and philosophical perspectives that have enriched public debate and cultural discussion.

Specific Cultural Contributions

Immigration has contributed to the cultural richness of the United States in many ways. In the kitchen, immigrants introduced a variety of dishes that have become staples of American culinary culture. Italian pizzas, Mexican tacos, and Japanese sushi have become national favorites, illustrating how immigrant food traditions have been integrated and transformed into essential elements of American culinary identity.

In music, the contributions of immigrants have been equally significant. Jazz, for example, was heavily influenced by African and African-American musical traditions, creating a musical genre that is emblematic of the United States. Rock and roll were also shaped by African, European, and Latin American influences. Immigrants brought instruments and musical styles that merged to create new genres that resonate around the world.

The visual arts have also benefited from the contributions of immigrants. Artists from Europe, Asia, and Latin America have enriched the American art scene with diverse styles and unique perspectives. Art galleries, theaters, and studios have seen significant contributions from immigrant artists who have introduced new techniques, concepts, and forms of artistic expression.

b. – How diversity is both an asset and a challenge for host countries

The diversity generated by immigration is an invaluable asset, but it also poses significant challenges to host countries. Understanding this duality is essential to fully appreciate the benefits and complexities associated with immigration.

The benefits of diversity

1. Innovation and creativity: Diversity fosters innovation by bringing together people with different experiences, perspectives, and skills. Diverse teams are often more creative and able to solve problems in original ways. Companies and institutions that embrace diversity benefit from new ideas and innovative solutions that can help them remain competitive in the global marketplace.

2. Social Cohesion and Cultural Enrichment: Cultural diversity contributes to a richer, more vibrant society. Exchanges between different cultures promote mutual understanding, respect for differences and social cohesion. Cultural festivals, diverse cuisines and artistic events are examples of how diversity enriches everyday life.

3. Economic development: Immigrants bring skills and talents that can help fill labor shortages and stimulate economic growth. They create businesses, generate jobs, and contribute to increased productivity. Diversified economies are often more resilient and adaptable to economic change.

The challenges of diversity

1. Cultural and social tensions: Diversity can sometimes lead to cultural and social tensions. Differences in values, traditions and lifestyles can lead to conflict or misunderstanding. It is important to promote integration policies that foster intercultural dialogue and mutual understanding to minimize these tensions.

2. Inequalities and discrimination: Despite the positive contributions of immigrants, some groups may face inequalities and discrimination. Racial and ethnic prejudice, economic inequalities and barriers to access can limit the opportunities available to some immigrants. It is essential to address these issues through fair and inclusive policies.

3. Integration and assimilation: The integration of immigrants into the host society can be complex. Challenges include learning the language, adapting to social norms, and accessing essential services. Integration programs must be well designed to help immigrants overcome these obstacles and fully integrate into their new community.

c. – Testimonials from immigrants who have found their place in various Sectors of American society

The stories of immigrants who have successfully integrated and thrived in the United States illustrate the positive contributions of immigration and show how challenges can be overcome. These stories are a source of inspiration and a powerful reminder of the opportunities that diversity offers.

Testimonials from the Business Sector

Carlos Rivera, Entrepreneur: Carlos, a Mexican immigrant, came to the United States with a simple dream: to open a restaurant. After years of hard work and saving, he founded El Camino, a restaurant that has become a popular gathering place in his community. His restaurant doesn't just serve food; it has become a place to celebrate Mexican cultural traditions. Carlos is now a role model for other immigrants who want to become entrepreneurs, showing how passion and determination can lead to success.

Aisha Mohamed, NGO Founder: Originally from Sudan, Aisha founded a nongovernmental organization dedicated to helping refugees and immigrants. Drawing on her personal experience of exile, she created a support network to help newcomers find housing, jobs and community resources. Her work has had a profound impact on the lives of many immigrants, facilitating their integration and enabling them to rebuild their lives in the United States.

Testimonials from the Technology Sector

Ravi Patel, Software Engineer: Ravi is a software engineer who came from India to work in Silicon Valley. His technical expertise and ability to work in a multicultural environment have made him a valuable asset to his company. Ravi is also involved in diversity initiatives in the technology sector, demonstrating how the skills and perspectives of immigrants can contribute to innovation and success in cutting-edge industries.

Mei Ling, Researcher: Mei Ling is a biotechnology researcher from China. Her work has led to significant advances in the field of gene therapy. As a scientist, she has brought a unique perspective and contributed to discoveries that have the potential to transform healthcare. Mei Ling is an example of how foreign talent can play a key role in scientific and medical research in the United States.

Testimonials from the Arts and Culture Sector

Amara Diallo, visual artist: Amara, a Senegalese artist, uses her art to explore and express themes of identity and diaspora. Her work has been exhibited in galleries across the U.S. and has been praised for its emotional depth and unique perspective. Her work illustrates how the artistic contributions of immigrants enrich American culture and foster greater cross-cultural understanding.

David Cohen, Director: David, an Israeli immigrant, has become an acclaimed Hollywood director. His films tackle complex issues of culture and identity, offering fresh perspectives on universal themes. His contributions have not only broadened the horizons of American cinema, but also demonstrated how international experiences and voices can enrich the nation's cultural landscape.

Immigration and diversity are essential elements of the American identity. Successive waves of immigration have enriched America's culture, economy, and society in profound and significant ways. While diversity presents challenges, it also offers invaluable opportunities for innovation, social cohesion, and economic development. Testimonials from immigrants who have found their place in diverse fields demonstrate how the contributions of immigrants can transform and enrich American society. By recognizing and celebrating these contributions, we can promote mutual understanding and build a more inclusive and dynamic society.

CHAPTER SEVEN

CONSCIENCE THAT THE AMERICAN DREAM DOESN'T BELONG TO ALL OF US

I went in search of America, and on the one hand it smiles at me, and on the other hand I see an America that humiliates my people. The American dream, this concept of a better life, prosperity and success within everyone's reach, gives me access, but it seems to have a dominant color. Although America was built on immigration, there's no denying that this dream is tinged with racial inequality. For some, the doors are wide open; for others, they remain stubbornly closed, locked by prejudice and discrimination deeply rooted in society. America as a nation must face this uncomfortable truth: not all immigrants are treated equally. The American dream, which is supposed to be universal, is often reserved for a privileged elite, for those whose skin color matches the ideal we have constructed of that dream. The rest of us - Blacks, Latinos, Haitians - struggle in the shadows, trying to integrate into a society that erects visible and invisible barriers.

A. – The evolution of the "American Dream" for immigrants in the current context

The "American Dream" has long been the beacon that has guided millions of immigrants to America's shores, promising a better life, unlimited opportunity, and a prosperous future. This dream is based on the idea that through hard work, determination, and perseverance, anyone, regardless of background, can achieve success. In today's context, however, this dream is confronted with complex and sometimes discouraging realities.

1. – The American Dream: A historical vision

Historically, the American Dream has been shaped by ideals of opportunity, freedom, and success. Early immigrants were attracted by the promise of a land of unlimited opportunity, far from the restrictions and inequalities of their homelands. The great waves of immigration in the 19th and early 20th centuries saw individuals and families struggling to build new lives in a country undergoing rapid economic expansion.

For these immigrants, the American Dream was embodied in the opportunity to buy a home, secure a stable job, and provide a better future for their children. The success of figures such as Andrew Carnegie and Henry Ford, who came from humble beginnings but became symbols of success, reinforced the appeal of this dream.

2. – The American Dream tested in modern times

Today, the American Dream has evolved in response to economic, social, and political change. For modern immigrants, the dream is no longer just about economic prosperity, but also about social integration, recognition, and equality. Today's challenges include growing economic inequality, global economic fluctuations, and the rise of nationalist sentiments that can threaten the opportunities promised by the American Dream.

The promise of a better life often seems out of reach for many immigrants, who face obstacles such as discrimination, unequal access to basic services, and precarious working conditions. Struggles to obtain immigration documents, lengthy processes to gain citizenship, and restrictive immigration policies have made the American Dream a more arduous quest.

3. – The effects of economic and political crises

Economic recessions, political crises, and changes in immigration policy have also affected perceptions of the American Dream. The Great Recession of 2008, for example, exacerbated immigrants' economic difficulties by making it harder for them to find stable, well-paying jobs. Immigration restrictions imposed by recent administrations have also created a climate of uncertainty and disillusionment among immigrants.

Family separation policies, mass deportations, and a reluctance to grant protected status or residency have created a hostile environment for many immigrants, making the American Dream an increasingly distant vision. In response to these challenges, immigrants often must demonstrate remarkable resilience and ingenuity to navigate a complex and often unfavorable system.

B. – The Paradox of a country built by immigrants but at times seemingly hostile to immigrants

As we saw already, by its very nature, the United States is a country built on immigration. American history is marked by the contributions of immigrants who built the country, brought new ideas, and enriched the culture. However, there is a profound paradox between this historical reality and the sometimes-hostile attitudes toward immigrants at certain times in American history.

1. – The historical paradox

The paradox lies in the fact that the United States has been shaped by successive waves of immigrants who have played a crucial role in the country's development. The infrastructure, businesses, cultural institutions, and technological innovations that have made the United States a global superpower are largely the result of immigrant contributions.

Despite this historical reality, there have been periods of intolerance and suspicion toward immigrants. In the late 19th and early 20th centuries, for example, immigrants from southern and eastern Europe faced racial prejudice and restrictive policies. More recently, immigrants from the Middle East, Africa, and Latin America have also been targets of discriminatory policies and hate speech.

2. – Anti-immigration policies

Anti-immigration policies, which emerge in response to economic crises, security concerns, or demographic shifts, often reflect feelings of fear and mistrust. Political debates on immigration are often polarized, with voices advocating restrictive policies and others defending the rights of immigrants and the need to reform the immigration system.

Policies such as border walls, travel bans, and deportation measures have fueled a climate of hostility toward immigrants, despite the fact that these same immigrants contribute significantly to the economy and society. At the heart of this paradox is the contrast between stated values of opportunity and inclusion and often restrictive actual policies.

3. – The influence of political and media discourse

Political and media discourses also play a crucial role in the perception of immigration. Negative media portrayals, populist political rhetoric and stereotypes can exacerbate anti-immigrant sentiments. These representations create misperceptions about immigrants, portraying them as threats rather than positive contributors to society.

Immigration policies based on fear and mistrust, often exacerbated by misinformation campaigns and scaremongering, fuel a climate of division and conflict. This contributes to a cycle in which restrictive policies are reinforced by hostile attitudes, making the American Dream even more elusive for many immigrants.

C. – Reflections on the Search for a better future and possible disillusionment

The search for a better future is at the heart of the immigrant experience, but it is often accompanied by disillusionment with the complex and sometimes disappointing reality of the United States. The high hopes of immigrants are met with practical and emotional challenges that can call into question the promise of the American Dream.

1. – Immigrant hopes and expectations

Immigrants often arrive with high expectations and an optimistic vision of what the United States can offer them. They seek economic opportunity, a better quality of life, and a safer environment for their families. The American Dream, as perceived abroad, is associated with values of freedom, equal opportunity, and prosperity.

These expectations are fueled by success stories, testimonials from successful immigrants, and cultural representations that portray the U.S. as a place of limitless opportunity. Immigrants are willing to work hard, make sacrifices, and overcome obstacles to achieve this dream.

2. – Disillusionment and obstacles

However, the reality can be very different from the ideal. Obstacles such as discrimination, economic inequality, and integration challenges can turn immigrants' hopes into disillusionment. The difficulty of finding stable employment, the high cost of living, and language barriers can make realizing the American Dream much more complicated than expected.

Immigrants may also encounter institutional barriers, such as the complex bureaucracy involved in obtaining visas or residency status. Initial expectations may be disappointed by a reality that seems much harder to navigate. Precarious living conditions, difficult access to health care and education, and a sense of exclusion can lead to a sense of failure and frustration.

3. – Overcoming disillusionment

Despite these challenges, many immigrants find ways to overcome disillusionment and build successful lives in the United States. Resilience, determination, and support are key factors in helping immigrants overcome obstacles and realize their aspirations.

Community organizations, support groups, and social networks play a critical role in providing resources and facilitating integration. Immigrants who are able to connect with mentors, access job training, and participate actively in their community are often more likely to succeed despite challenges.

The American Dream, as inspiring and promising as it is, faces complex challenges in the current context. The evolution of the dream, the paradox of hostile attitudes toward immigration, and the potential for disillusionment highlight the complex realities of the immigrant experience. Immigrants continue to seek for a better future but often face significant obstacles to realizing their aspirations. By recognizing these challenges and working toward a more inclusive and equitable society, it is possible to reconcile the American Dream with reality and ensure that the promise of opportunity remains accessible to all.

Yet there is a troubling paradox between the fundamental role of immigrants in building the country and the sometimes-hostile attitudes toward immigration. This paradox reflects deep-seated tensions in American society and raises important questions about the country's national identity and core values.

4. – A nation built on immigration

In order to prove the paradox, let's recall once again that, since its beginnings, the United States has been shaped by the contributions of other peoples and immigrants since the War of Independence. American infrastructure, industry, and culture bear the mark of successive waves of immigrants who brought their skills, ideas, and determination. The country's rapid economic growth and cultural innovation are largely attributed to the contributions of its diverse immigrant communities.

Immigrants have played a key role in building the nation's infrastructure, creating new businesses, and enriching American culture. The contributions of immigrants are evident in technology, the arts, science, and many other fields. Their impact is undeniable and an integral part of American history and success.

5. – Hostile attitudes toward immigration

Despite these essential contributions, attitudes toward immigration have often been characterized by intolerance and suspicion. Anti-immigrant policies and populist rhetoric reflect feelings of fear and suspicion. Negative media portrayals, stereotypes, and alarmist political campaigns have exacerbated these feelings and created a climate of hostility toward immigrants.

Restrictive policies such as border walls, travel bans, and deportation policies illustrate this paradox. These policies are often motivated by security or economic concerns but ignore the positive contributions and fundamental rights of immigrants. The contrast between inclusive values and restrictive policies creates a conflict between the country's stated ideals and its actual actions.

6. – The influence of political and media discourse

Political and media discourses play a crucial role in the perception of immigration. Negative portrayals of immigrants, hate speech and stereotypes fuel anti-immigrant sentiments. Policies based on fear and mistrust are often reinforced by media narratives that portray immigrants as threats rather than positive contributors to society.

Political campaigns that use alarmist rhetoric about immigration can exacerbate divisions and reinforce hostile attitudes. Such rhetoric creates a climate of mistrust and conflict that makes it even harder for immigrants to achieve the American dream. Political polarization over immigration reflects deep-seated tensions in American society and challenges the nation's core values.

CHAPTER EIGHT

CONSCIENCE OF THE FUTURE THAT IS OURS

Over the next twenty years, the situation of immigrants in the United States will undoubtedly be marked by profound transformations as well as persistent challenges. The political, economic, and social issues surrounding immigration will continue to shape the lives of millions of people, both those seeking refuge and those struggling to maintain a position of influence in an ever-changing society.

On the one hand, immigration will remain a key driver of economic and demographic growth in the United States. Immigrants will continue to bring their dynamism, creativity, and skills to help renew the country's social and economic fabric. In key sectors such as health care, technology, agriculture, and services, immigrant workers will continue to fill critical gaps and underpin American prosperity. Yet despite these undeniable contributions, debates about their place in society will remain polarized.

On the other hand, waves of immigration will continue to be influenced by global factors such as climate change, conflict, and rising inequality. In particular, climate-induced migration will multiply as populations flee regions devastated by increasingly frequent natural disasters. This phenomenon could exacerbate political tensions over the management of migratory flows, especially as the question of national identity will remain at the heart of political concerns.

Progress could also be made on migrants' rights, but not without resistance. Pressure for comprehensive immigration reform, including the regularization of undocumented immigrants, could increase. There is hope that civil rights movements and immigrant coalitions will succeed in moving laws toward greater inclusiveness in the coming decades. However, reactionary forces armed with xenophobic rhetoric will do their utmost to halt this progress by rekindling fears of the "other" and capitalizing on economic insecurity to justify exclusionary policies.

What's more, the issue of immigration will increasingly be linked to the issue of race. Immigrants of color, in particular, will continue to face double discrimination: as foreigners and as members of racial minorities. The rise of racial justice movements, however, could play a crucial role in making these struggles visible and in building new solidarities among black, Latino, Asian, and other minority communities.

Younger generations of immigrants born or raised in the United States will also play a critical role in the country's future. They will be the bearers of new, more nuanced and diverse narratives about immigration, and they will invest in civic and political life with renewed energy. Twenty years from now, these children of immigrants could be at the helm of institutions, major corporations, or even politics, redefining America in their own image.

But all this will only be possible if American society can overcome its internal divisions and recognize that immigration, far from being a threat, is a source of wealth and renewal. The future of immigrants in the United States will depend on our ability to forge a discourse that values diversity, to build inclusive institutions, and to meet basic human needs for justice and dignity. If we fail, we risk perpetuating cycles of discrimination and marginalization. But if we succeed, we could finally give substance to an America that truly embodies its ideals of liberty and equality for all.

Over the next twenty years, immigration will reflect the choices we make as a society. In the face of these challenges, we must choose the path of empathy, inclusion, and solidarity, because that's where our common humanity lies.

A. – How to imagine immigration reconciled with American values: proposals for immigration policy reform

Immigration is at the center of political and social debates in the United States, but it should also be at the center of efforts to build a more just and inclusive society. To reconcile immigration with American values of freedom, equality, and justice, it is essential to rethink and reform current immigration policies. Here are some suggestions for creating an immigration system that reflects these values while responding to today's challenges.

1. – Reform the visa and residency system

The current visa and residency system is complex and often restrictive, which can discourage potential immigrants and create barriers for those who wish to make a positive contribution to American society. Reform of the system should include

— Simplify access to visas: Make it easier for skilled workers, entrepreneurs, and international students to obtain visas. A point system could be used to assess applicants' skills and potential contributions.

— A clear path to permanent residency: Provide a clearer, more accessible path to permanent residency and citizenship for immigrants who contribute positively to American society. This would include measures to avoid excessive delays and bureaucratic hurdles.

— More humane family reunification policies: Reduce delays and restrictions on family reunification so that families can be reunited more quickly. Supporting family unity is essential to maintaining the cohesion of immigrant communities.

2. – A human rights-based approach

Immigration policies should be based on respect for human rights and the dignity of the individual. This implies

— Improving detention conditions: Ensure that conditions in immigration detention centers respect humanitarian standards and the rights of detainees. Detention should be avoided wherever possible, especially for families and children.

— Equitable access to services: Ensure that all migrants, regardless of status, have access to essential services such as health, education, and legal assistance. Access to social services is critical to the integration and well-being of immigrants.

— End family separation policies: End policies that result in the separation of immigrant families, particularly border separation practices. The preservation of family units must be a priority.

3. – Promote Civic and Political Participation

Immigrants play an important role in American society and should be given more opportunities to participate actively in civic and political life. This includes

- Facilitate access to citizenship: Simplify the naturalization process to encourage immigrants to become citizens and participate fully in political life. Citizenship preparation courses and civic integration programs can be established.

- Promote political representation: Promote immigrant representation in local, state, and federal political institutions. Inclusive and representative politics better reflect the diversity of American society.

B. – Advocate for a more inclusive and humane society in which immigrants are seen not as a threat but as key agents of progress.

To build a more inclusive and humane society, it's critical to change perceptions of immigrants and recognize their essential role in the nation's progress. Here are some calls to make this vision a reality:

1. – Valuing Immigrant Contributions

- Immigrants make significant contributions to the U.S. economy, culture, and society. It's important to value these contributions and include them in the public discourse:

- Highlight immigrant success stories: Highlight immigrant success stories and contributions in a variety of fields, including business, academia, culture, and public service. These stories demonstrate how immigrants enrich and shape American society.

- Celebrate cultural diversity: Celebrate the cultural diversity brought by immigrants through events, festivals, and educational programs. Diversity is a force for cultural richness and innovation.

2. – Education and Awareness

Education and awareness play a crucial role in changing perceptions and reducing prejudice:

- Intercultural education programs: Introduce intercultural education programs in schools and communities to promote mutual understanding and respect. Education is about the contributions of immigrants and the benefits of diversity can reduce stereotypes and prejudice.

   – Awareness campaigns: Launch awareness campaigns about the realities and challenges faced by immigrants and the benefits they bring to society. Personal testimonies and case studies can help humanize the debate on immigration.

3. – Promoting Social Integration

The successful integration of immigrants into society is essential to creating an inclusive environment:

   – Community integration programs: Establish integration programs that help immigrants adjust to their new lives, including language classes, job training, and support services. Effective integration facilitates immigrants' full and equal participation in society.

   – Support local initiatives: Encourage local initiatives that promote immigrant integration and social cohesion. Partnerships between community organizations, local governments, and businesses can play an important role in these efforts.

C. – Urging the U.S. to help small countries develop to keep their citizens at home

For decades, the United States has chosen to turn its back on Latin America and the Caribbean, preferring destabilization and interventionism to genuine cooperation. By exerting a destructive influence on the region, it has encouraged the emergence of fragile, unstable, and often authoritarian regimes while neglecting the social and economic development of these nations. By seeking to consolidate their power in the region, they have diverted attention from the suffering of neighboring peoples and fueled political and economic crises in countries that are now becoming ungovernable.

Haiti is the most poignant example. It has been suffocating under the weight of foreign intervention and interference. Instead of supporting Haiti in its quest for stability and development, the United States has chosen to keep the country in perpetual dependence, undermining its sovereignty and its chances for prosperity.

By prioritizing short-term economic interests, the United States has helped create pockets of instability that are now spiraling out of control. Nations once influenced by U.S. power now face waves of violence, forced migration, and collective despair. In the long run, this short-sighted policy has created enemies where there could have been allies. By turning its back on these countries, the United States has allowed the roots of injustice to grow even deeper.

It's time to acknowledge this mistake. All of America, from north to south, is bound by a common destiny. If the United States continues to ignore the humanitarian, social, and economic crises of its neighbors, it will continue to feed the vicious cycle of instability. You must choose the path of cooperation, of genuine aid, of justice. History does not forgive those who abandon their neighbors, and the future cannot be built on the ashes of nations weakened by the power of one.

So, to address the root causes of immigration, the U.S must play an active role in supporting the development of small immigrant-sending countries. Here are some suggestions for supporting this effort:

1. – Partnerships for Development

The United States can partner with immigrants' countries of origin to promote economic and social development:

- Invest in economic development: Support investment projects in key sectors such as education, health, infrastructure, and agriculture. investments can help create employment opportunities and improve living conditions in countries of origin.

- Knowledge Exchange Programs: Establish knowledge and technology exchange programs to strengthen local capabilities and foster innovation. These programs can include training, workshops, and business-to-business collaboration.

2. – Strengthening Democratic Institutions

The United States can support efforts to strengthen democratic institutions and promote good governance:

- Technical assistance and training: Provide technical assistance and training to government institutions and civil society organizations in developing countries. Strengthening institutional capacity contributes to better governance and political stability.

- Promoting Human Rights and Justice: Promoting human rights and justice reforms to ensure that fundamental rights are protected and that justice systems are fair. Promoting social justice contributes to more stable and prosperous societies.

3. – Supporting Economic Resilience

The United States can help developing countries diversify their economies and build resilience to crises:

- Support programs for small businesses: Establish programs to support small businesses and local entrepreneurs to stimulate economic growth and job creation. Small businesses play a key role in local economic development.

- Humanitarian and crisis response: Provide humanitarian and crisis response assistance to communities affected by natural disasters, conflicts, and economic crises. Rapid and effective assistance can help stabilize and rebuild affected regions.

In envisioning an immigration system consistent with American values, it is critical to reform immigration policies to make them more inclusive and humane. By valuing the contributions of immigrants, promoting education and awareness, and supporting international development efforts, the United States can build a more just and prosperous society for all. Efforts to support the development of countries of origin are essential to addressing the root causes of immigration and creating opportunities for those who wish to remain at home. By taking these steps, the United States can reaffirm its commitment to the core values of freedom, equality, and justice, while building a more inclusive and sustainable future for all.

When Haiti became the world's first black republic in 1804, it wasn't a selfish act. We did it not just for ourselves, but for all the oppressed, forgotten, and neglected of the world. We thought of those whose voices were silenced, those whose dignity was scorned. We knew what it meant to be deprived of freedom, and that's why we decided to share what was most precious to us: our freedom.

We opened our borders to all lovers of freedom, to all those who sought refuge from injustice. Haiti was not just a territory, it was a symbol, a country of resistance, an empire of freedom. By breaking our chains, we wanted to inspire those who, like us, were fighting for their right to exist.

Our revolution was not just a rebellion against oppression; it was a message to the world: the weak, the marginalized, and those forgotten on the margins of history had their place in the dream of freedom. For our independence wasn't just ours. It was the promise of a future where everyone, regardless of race or condition, could rise with dignity.

This is the mission, the commitment we have made to ourselves and the world. Haiti, in all its suffering, in all its struggle, remains a land of courage, hope, and freedom for those whom the world rejects. We have made mistakes, and it is true that we have been misled. We have failed ourselves and all those who suffer around the world. We bear the burden of our own suffering, but also of our inability to alleviate the pain of the poor, the widow, and the orphan. That's why the world has always needed Haiti. Because in Haiti lies a mission greater than us, to embody compassion and justice for the most vulnerable.

CONCLUSION

Universal Conscience

The systematic persecution of Haitians today, in its violence and inhumanity, is reminiscent of that which Hitler orchestrated against the Jews during one of the darkest periods of history. While the contexts and times may be different, the essence of this persecution remains the same: a blind, irrational hatred that refuses to recognize the dignity and humanity of a group of people and accuses us of importing the Third World into the United States. Since when have we lost the right to live in the land where the blood of our ancestors was shed for freedom?

Haitians, like Jews in the past, are targeted for reasons that go beyond the simple fact of immigration. They are demonized, stigmatized, and reduced to stereotypes that in no way reflect the richness of their culture, their history, or their contributions to society. Like Hitler, who used the Jews as a scapegoat to justify Germany's ills, some politicians and leaders today exploit Haitians as symbols of economic crisis, crime, and insecurity to foment fear and division.

This process of dehumanization and rejection has had devastating consequences. Despite their struggle for a better life, Haitians are denied their rights, turned back at the border, or imprisoned in detention centers in often inhumane conditions. Attempts are made to make them invisible as if their very existence were a threat. But behind these actions lies a darker truth: fear of the other, fear of what they represent.

Like the Jews under Hitler, Haitians are accused of everything and nothing, victims of a hatred that refuses to see their humanity. This is not just a question of immigration or migration policy; it's a question of basic human rights. Haitians have the right to live in peace, to be treated with dignity and respect, and to have the chance to build a future for their families.

The mistakes of the past must not be repeated. Silence in the face of injustice, in the face of persecution, allows hatred to grow and destroy. If we close our eyes today, we allow history to repeat itself. The people of Haiti deserve better. They deserve recognition of their humanity, not to be the target of systemic, organized violence.

It's time to say no to this hatred, denounce it forcefully, and remember that Haitians, just like Jews or any other persecuted people in history, have the right to live, thrive, and be treated with the respect that every human being deserves. The lessons of history are clear: when we choose to blame and persecute rather than understand and reach out, we are on the wrong track. We all have a collective responsibility to defend human dignity and to refuse to fall into the trap of blind hatred that has caused so much suffering in the past.

A final reflection on humanism, solidarity, and the importance of rethinking immigration not only in political terms but also in terms of a shared human conscience.

In the preceding chapters, we have explored the complexities of immigration in the American context, examined the challenges and opportunities it presents, and proposed ways forward for a more humane and just approach. As we move toward the conclusion of our reflections, it is crucial to emphasize that immigration cannot be viewed solely through the prism of government policies and strategies. Beyond the technical and legislative aspects, it goes to the heart of our humanity and collective solidarity. This conclusion seeks to deepen this perspective by examining immigration from the perspective of humanism, solidarity, and universal consciousness.

A. – Humanism as a basis for migration policy

Humanism, as a philosophy, values the dignity and rights of every human being, regardless of origin, nationality, or status. This perspective is particularly relevant to the reform of migration policies. Too often, discussions on immigration are dominated by economic and political arguments, neglecting the human and ethical dimensions of the issue. Putting humanism back at the center of immigration debates is crucial to ensuring that policies are not only effective but also fair and respectful of human dignity.

1. – Respect for human dignity

Migration policies must be rooted in respect for human dignity. Every individual, whether citizen or migrant, deserves to be treated with respect and fairness. This means

- Decent living and detention conditions: Ensure that the conditions in which immigrants live, particularly in detention centers, meet international human rights standards. Inhuman or degrading conditions should not be tolerated.

- Access to justice and basic services: Ensure that all migrants have access to legal, medical, and social services. Immigrants should be able to enjoy their fundamental rights regardless of their status.

- Recognizing the contributions of immigrants: Valuing the contribution of immigrants to society, the economy, and culture. Their contribution is often underestimated or ignored, and it is important to recognize and fully value it.

2. – Promoting Equality and Integration

Humanism calls for the promotion of equality and integration of immigrants in the host society. This includes

- Equal opportunities: Implementing policies that provide equal opportunities for all, regardless of background. This includes access to education, employment, and other economic opportunities.

- Effective integration programs: Developing programs that help immigrants fully integrate into society. These programs should include language courses, vocational training, and initiatives to promote cultural exchange.

- Combat discrimination: Implement policies against discrimination based on migration status. Prejudices and stereotypes must be addressed through awareness campaigns and diversity training.

B. – Solidarity as a guiding principle

Solidarity is a fundamental principle that should guide our actions towards migrants. It implies a mutual commitment to support those in need and to work together to build a more just society. In the context of immigration, solidarity takes the form of

1. – A coordinated humanitarian response

Migration crises require an internationally coordinated humanitarian response:

– International cooperation: Countries must work together to address migration crises, sharing responsibilities and providing humanitarian assistance to displaced persons. International solidarity is essential to address the global challenges posed by migration.

– Supporting countries of origin: Providing assistance to migrants' countries of origin to help them improve living conditions and stabilize political and economic situations. Support for these countries can help reduce the root causes of immigration.

– Sharing responsibility fairly: Countries must share the responsibility for receiving immigrants fairly, so as not to overburden certain countries or regions. Solidarity among nations is essential to ensure fair treatment of immigrants.

2. – Promoting social cohesion

Promoting social cohesion is an important dimension of solidarity:

– Community initiatives: Support local initiatives that promote meetings and exchanges between immigrants and members of the host community. Community projects can strengthen social ties and promote mutual understanding.

– Promoting intercultural dialogues: Create spaces for dialogue among different cultures and ethnic groups. These dialogues can help overcome misunderstandings and build a more inclusive society.

– Supporting immigrant families and communities: Provide specific support to immigrant families and communities, taking into account their particular needs. Supporting families is essential for their integration and well-being.

C. – Universal Consciousness as Horizon

Finally, the notion of universal consciousness calls for a deeper reflection on our common humanity. By viewing immigration through the prism of universal consciousness, we recognize that every individual, regardless of where he or she was born, belongs to a global community.

1. – Collective Responsibility

We have a collective responsibility to those who seek a better life elsewhere. This means

- Accepting the consequences of migration policies: Recognize that migration policies have a significant impact on human lives. National and international decisions must be guided by principles of justice and compassion.

- Promote global development policies: Promote development policies aimed at reducing economic and social inequalities on a global scale. Sustainable and equitable development is essential to addressing the root causes of migration.

- Cultivate a culture of compassion: Cultivate a culture of empathy and understanding on a global scale. Individuals and communities must see themselves not only as national actors but also as global citizens.

2. – Rethinking human values

Rethinking human values in the context of immigration means reassessing our priorities and principles:

- Humanity and solidarity: redefining the values of our society to reflect humanity and solidarity with others. Humanist values must guide our policies and attitudes toward immigrants.

- Equity and social justice: Ensure that the principles of equity and social justice are integrated into migration policies and corporate practices. Social justice must be at the heart of the response to the challenges of migration.

- Respect for human rights: Promote respect for human rights for all, regardless of migration status. Basic rights must be protected and respected in all circumstances.

3. – Building a common future

Building a shared future means working together to create a society in which everyone can thrive:

- Create opportunities for all: Develop policies and initiatives that provide opportunities for all individuals, whether immigrants or citizens. Equal access to opportunities is essential to building a prosperous and inclusive society.

- Promoting international cooperation: Encourage cooperation among nations to address global challenges related to immigration. Joint efforts can help solve complex problems and promote a more equitable global society.

- Promoting Peace and Security: Working to promote peace and security around the world. Political and economic stability are essential to reducing forced migration and creating an environment in which people can thrive.

One absolute truth remains: no matter where we come from, even if we immigrate to the United States, our fate will always be linked in one way or another to that of our country of origin, especially Haiti. We carry within us the history, the sufferings and the hopes of the country in which we were born. Leaving does not mean fleeing this reality, but taking it with us, in our hearts and minds. This invisible link shapes our ambitions, influences the way we are perceived, and colors our experiences in this new world.

When our country goes through a crisis - whether economic, political, or social - it follows us, even thousands of miles away. In the United States, our success is sometimes viewed through the prism of stereotypes associated with our origins. The image of our country, its struggles and stigmas, become burdens that we often have to carry in spite of ourselves. The media speaks of "poor countries" or "nations in crisis", and these narratives sometimes overshadow the path we're trying to take here.

But this connection to our homeland is also a strength. It reminds us of where we came from and why we embarked on this journey. It is in this duality that we find our resilience. We are building a future elsewhere, but we remain attached to a past that gives us meaning an identity. We work hard not only for ourselves, but also to give something better to future generations, and perhaps even to our homeland.

So while our fate in the U.S. depends in part on the fate of our homeland, it's also a chance to turn that interdependence into something powerful. By succeeding here, we can contribute to hope, to rebuilding, to pride in our roots. Our successes then become not only our own, but those of a people, a history and a future that we continue to write, even from afar.

After all, what are we, immigrants from the United States? We are the dreamers, the bridge builders between two worlds, those who carry the weight of hope on our shoulders. We are those who have left behind entire lives, families, and homes to seek elsewhere what our homeland could no longer offer: security, opportunity, a dignified future.

We are the promise of tomorrow, the quiet force shaping America today. Our hands build its skyscrapers, our talents enrich its industries, our cultures color its streets. Yet we are often invisible. Invisible in the political discourses, in the media, in the narratives that define this nation. But silently, we continue to move forward, to persevere, to believe.

What are we if not resilient souls? We've crossed oceans, deserts and borders, not only for ourselves, but for those we've left behind. Every step we take in this foreign land is an act of courage, a cry for freedom, a commitment to our children to give them a better life, a life we sometimes only dreamed of.

We are fighters, resilient in the face of adversity, bearers of hope, even when everything seems to tell us we won't make it. We face obstacles, misunderstanding and marginalization with the strength of a past that nothing can erase. Our stories are not just our own, but those of millions of people throughout history who have helped make this country what it is today.

We are the guardians of diversity; the very essence of what America has represented since its founding. We carry cultures, languages, and histories that enrich this country. Every accent, every dish, every piece of music we bring makes the American mosaic vibrate a little more.

We are survivors, but more than that, we are creators of opportunity. As immigrants, we are not mere passengers in this country, we are its architects, shaping the future of this nation at every turn with our dreams, our work, and our indomitable resilience.

And for us Haitians, we are also, and above all, contributors to a better host country and builders of the country in which we were born.

It is imperative that people take their destiny into their own hands and rise up with strength and determination to build a better future for their citizens. For too long, entire nations have been at the mercy of injustice, insecurity, and exploitative and oppressive systems. But it's time for this era to end. The power to transform society is not in the hands of a few but in the hands of all those who seek freedom, equality, and dignity.

Every citizen deserves to live in a country where justice, peace and security prevail. No child should grow up in fear, no family should be broken by violence, and no individual should be silenced by injustice. When people unite, when they refuse to give in to fate, that's when true transformation happens.

It is our duty as communities to take concrete action, to organize, and to resist injustice in all its forms. History has shown us that the most profound changes come from the people and that revolutions are born in the hearts of those who refuse to accept oppression. And it is this spirit that we must rekindle.

It's not just about demanding rights, it's about building a future where everyone can thrive, and where citizens feel protected, listened to, and respected. Leaders are only temporary custodians of what we as a people have the power to create and defend. It is time to take back that power, redefine our common destiny, and give every human being the life of dignity they deserve.

Destiny is not something you suffer, it's something you build. And it's up to us to build it, to guarantee our children a world where justice and security are realities, not privileges reserved for the few. Today, Haiti stands at a historic crossroads, a rare opportunity to rise from the ashes like a phoenix after years of suffering and despair. Long scarred by poverty, instability, and insecurity, the country now has the chance to turn the page, rewrite its history, and reinvent itself for a brighter future.

This renaissance will not be easy. The challenges are immense, but not insurmountable. Haiti has the strength of a resilient people capable of overcoming the worst trials. Haitians have withstood storms, exploitation, and natural and man-made disasters. Today, that same strength must be mobilized to build a country worthy of its revolutionary heritage, a country that is free, just and prosperous.

We have the opportunity to lay the foundations for a new society in which every citizen has access to education, decent health care, security and economic opportunity. This is not a time for lament, but a time for action. It is time for Haiti to take its destiny into its own hands, to unite and chart a course toward true national redemption.

The world is watching Haiti, and many still doubt its ability to recover. But it is in these moments of doubt that nations transcend themselves. Change begins with the conviction that anything is possible and that every Haitian, by standing up and refusing to give in to fatalism, can contribute to this rebirth.

Today, more than ever, Haiti can once again become a symbol of hope, courage and rebirth. The time has come to write a new chapter in which unity and solidarity will be the foundations of a bright future worthy of the greatness of this people.

In closing, I'll say this: The American Constitution begins with these powerful words: « We, the people… » Words that resonate throughout history, a universal call to unity, freedom, and human dignity. But this "people" has never been homogeneous. From the beginning, it was made up of British descendants and immigrants from Europe, all of whom came in successive waves of immigration, bringing with them their hopes, their dreams, and their desire to build a better life.

This founding text established a fundamental principle: every person who treads this earth with a dream of freedom will find his or her place to contribute to a "more perfect union". It's an absolute truth: America's promise, its very essence, is to welcome those fleeing oppression, poverty, and war, and offer them a chance to prosper and become full members of this great nation.

Today, it's painful to realize that America, once the land of welcome, seems to have turned its back on its own roots. Immigrants, once a source of pride, have become a burden in the eyes of some. This country, built on the hands and hearts of countless immigrants, seems to have forgotten that it owes them everything.

America, which once counted on its immigrants as its lifeblood, now seems to count on them as a burden. Yet the dreams of immigrants past and present are the same: a quest for freedom, opportunity, and contribution to a common future. Every immigrant who sets foot in this country carries with them the promise of a renewed America, stronger, more diverse, and richer for its differences.

In the face of a fearful America, perhaps it's time to embrace this reality. To perhaps rewrite this story, to add a new phrase to this immortal Constitution: "We, the I-people too" - "I" for immigrant. Immigrants aren't just passengers in American history, they are key players, tireless builders of a dream that never stops reinventing itself.

Immigrants are not aliens to this nation. They are a reflection of what it has always been: a land of refuge, a place where the dream of freedom takes root. They are the invisible engine of a more perfect union, the very union the Constitution promised to build. It's time for America as a whole to remember its essence and to include in its foundation those who continue to keep its dream alive.

A. – Testimonials from other immigrants or experts on the Issue

Personal testimonies and expert perspectives shed valuable light on the reality of immigration and enrich our understanding of the challenges and successes associated with this phenomenon. Through these testimonies, we discover real human experiences that embody the many facets of immigration. These personal accounts and expert analysis allow us to grasp the complexity of immigration beyond the numbers and the politics.

1. – Immigrant Testimonies

Testimony of Maria, a Venezuelan immigrant

Maria, a young Venezuelan woman, left her country in the wake of Venezuela's devastating economic and political crisis. Her testimony illustrates the deep-seated motivations that drive people to leave their homes and seek refuge elsewhere.

"I left with the hope of finding a better future, far from the misery and political uncertainty that was tearing our country apart. My journey was long and difficult. When I arrived in the United States, I discovered a world radically different from what I had imagined. The language barrier was a major obstacle, and I had to work hard to adapt to new social and professional norms. Despite these challenges, I found a sense of community and solidarity in immigrant support groups. Today, although the road has been fraught with obstacles, I'm proud to be able to contribute to American society while honoring my Venezuelan roots.

Maria's story highlights the hopes and challenges that immigrants face as they leave their homelands and seek to integrate into a new society.

Testimony of Ahmed, a Syrian Refugee

Ahmed, a Syrian refugee, fled his war-torn country and sought refuge in Europe before settling in the United States. His experience illustrates the realities of forced migration and the struggle to rebuild a life in a host country.

"The war in Syria destroyed everything we had built. Fleeing my country was a difficult decision, but it was necessary to ensure my family's safety. Adjusting to a new environment was a huge challenge. I had to learn a new language, understand foreign laws and customs, and find a job in a competitive job market. However, I have also met a number of caring people who have helped me navigate this new world. My hope is to be able to give my children a life where they can dream without fear.

Ahmed's experience underscores the dimension of survival and resilience that often characterizes refugee journeys, as well as the crucial role of host communities in supporting new arrivals.

2. – Expert Insights

Expertise of Dr. Emily Johnson, Migration Policy Specialist

Dr. Emily Johnson, a migration policy expert, provides an academic perspective on the challenges and opportunities of immigration in the United States. Her research provides data and analysis that illuminate how migration policies affect the lives of immigrants and host communities.

"Immigration is a complex phenomenon that requires a balanced approach. Policies must be designed not only to address security and economic concerns but also to respect fundamental human rights. An approach based on inclusion and social justice can contribute to the successful integration of immigrants. Evidence shows that immigrants make significant contributions to the economy and culture, and it is essential to develop policies that maximize these contributions while supporting immigrants' integration".

Dr. Johnson's perspective reinforces the idea that migration policies must balance security and human rights while highlighting the positive contributions of immigrants. Expert Opinion by Dr. Luis Mendoza, Sociologist Specializing in Migration Issues

Dr. Luis Mendoza, a sociologist specializing in migration, analyzes the social and cultural impact of immigrants on host societies. His work provides information on intercultural dynamics and the impact of diversity on social cohesion.

"Immigration is a key factor in the cultural diversification that enriches host societies. But it can also create tensions if it is not managed inclusively. Encouraging intercultural exchange and promoting mutual understanding are key to preventing conflict and building a harmonious society. Policies must promote integration while respecting the cultural identities of immigrants. An approach based on dialogue and cooperation can turn challenges into opportunities to strengthen social cohesion.

Dr. Mendoza's insights highlight the importance of intercultural dialogue and inclusive diversity management in promoting a harmonious society.

B. – U.S. Immigration Data and Statistics

Data and statistics provide a quantitative overview of immigration trends and realities in the United States. They help to contextualize the personal testimonies and expert analysis and provide a comprehensive view of the impact of immigration on the country.

1. – General Immigration Trends

Immigrant Population: According to the Pew Research Center, there will be approximately 46 million immigrants in the United States in 2023, representing about 15% of the country's total population. This proportion is higher than in previous decades, underscoring the continued growth of immigration.

Origins of Immigrants: Immigrants to the United States come from many different parts of the world. In 2023, the top regions of origin for immigrants were Latin America (48%), Asia (30%), and Europe (10%). This geographic diversity reflects the many waves of immigration that have shaped American society.

Immigration status: Among immigrants, about 19 million are naturalized citizens, while 11 million are legal permanent residents. Approximately 4 million live in the United States without legal status, posing unique challenges to immigration policy and rights.

2. – Economic and Social Impacts

Economic Contributions: Immigrants play a key role in the U.S. economy. According to a study by the American Economic Review, immigrants contribute about 11% of the U.S. GDP and are particularly present in sectors such as technology, health care, and services. Their presence contributes to economic growth and job creation.

Starting businesses: Immigrants are also active entrepreneurs. According to a study by the Kauffman Foundation, about 25% of American businesses will be founded by immigrants by 2023. Their role in the entrepreneurial sector underscores their contribution to innovation and economic competitiveness.

Labor Market Impacts: Immigrants' impact on the labor market is complex. They often fill jobs that native-born workers do not want to fill while creating additional economic opportunities. Studies show that immigrants tend to fill positions in high-demand sectors such as construction, health care, and services.

3. – Challenges and Opportunities

Integration challenges: Data show that immigrants face a variety of integration challenges, including language barriers and access to education and social services. According to the Migration Policy Institute, about 30% of non-English-speaking immigrants have significant difficulty accessing basic services.

Opportunities for social cohesion: Integration initiatives, such as language training programs and employment support services, play a critical role in easing immigrants' transition into American society. Evidence suggests that well-designed programs can significantly improve employment and social integration outcomes.

In sum, immigrant and expert testimony, combined with immigration data and statistics, provide a rich and nuanced picture of the realities and impacts of immigration in the United States. These elements must be taken into account in formulating fair and effective immigration policies that respect human dignity while meeting the needs of society as a whole. Human experience and statistical analysis provide complementary perspectives that enrich our understanding of the challenges and opportunities associated with immigration and call for deeper reflection on how to build a more inclusive and supportive society.

ANNEX 2

SEPTEMBER 16TH DECLARATION Haitian people, Haitian youth.

Just because we as people are overcoming the greatest crisis in our history, does not mean that we don't have the right to live. Just because we're fleeing misery, and insecurity doesn't make us pestiferous. Just because we're among the least fortunate in the hemisphere doesn't make us a shithole country. In fact, there's no such thing as SH country; there are people who are struggling, and who have lost their way at certain points in their history. It's up to humanity to help them get back on their feet. If this is not done, humanity loses itself.

Today, unfortunately, it's our turn. This is the burden of our generation: to live in our time the sum of the errors and mistakes of past generations. And we are suffering. In truth, we suffer in our bones; we suffer from insecurity, from hunger, from the bankruptcy of our State; we suffer from the division of our nation. But not only that, we suffer from imperialism, from neo-colonization; yes, we suffer from shame, even humiliation, we suffer from the fact that we are on our knees. We suffer from fear.

We try to hide our shame, our unworthy situation, behind mockery and pride; we laugh at ourselves as we denigrate ourselves in order to survive. But in the face of the fear of what our children and grandchildren will become, we flee. We flee to the Dominican Republic, Brazil, Chile, Turkey, and here in the U.S., so that the only life each of us has can be invested in a better future, whatever the cost. From generation to generation, with each crisis, we flee, not counting those who have lost their lives in search of it in the Atlantic Ocean or in the forests of Central America. We've braved it all because, in the end, far from our core values, we've come to believe that the future lies elsewhere. Throughout human history, when not forcibly enslaved, people have always willingly sought the best elsewhere... Isn't that how we created countries, races and nations?

When Portugal faced the challenges of modernization after the Second World War, or when Greece recently struggled between a past that wouldn't go away and a future that wanted to impose itself in a fragile European context, no one said it was over for them. Why should it be over for us? Because when you see us today, you see ashes, so can't we be reborn? This is a misunderstanding of humanity, a misunderstanding of history. If one of us, or a foreigner, hastily accepts such a conclusion and chooses to treat us like cannibals, he is very much mistaken. Haiti is eternal and will always be reborn.

And while we've been impoverished and indulged in bad governance and corruption, it doesn't change the fact that here in America we brought "liberty for all" to the baptismal font in 1804; while the United States laid the foundations of freedom for one category of human beings in 1776. Indeed, it was not until 1865 that blacks in America were emancipated. And what emancipation? Together we founded the New World, and Haiti dared to say and prove that freedom has no color. We became the world's first black republic on the battlefield and earned our epaulets as abolitionists of the cynical industry of the day: slavery.

While we were paying off the double debt; while our country was divided in two, with the Northern Kingdom seeking to overthrow the Republic of the West, we were helping to bring about freedom for all in South America, as in the Old World. I shudder to say it because we believed that the New World had to be new in its values, in its vision of man and the world, and not a reproduction of the Old World with new masters. We've always been there, and we've always answered the call for freedom. We believed that in this new world, everyone had the right to happiness. And yet, Latin America, after all our help in the wars of liberation, reminded us at the Congress of Panama in 1826 that the color of our skin determines our destiny.

And even when we were occupied by the United States, we always lived with a single conscience: "Liberty is one for all." That is the foundation of our resilience. It is this awareness that in our suffering, in the face of such outrage, urges us not to be disappointed in America; that makes us understand that, as at home, there will always be executioners of freedom; those who can't imagine beautiful freedom in America without a subcategory of citizens. If it's not the African slaves and their descendants throughout American history, it's the immigrants of the 21st century.

It is this awareness that makes us hear the friendship of the great America, the real America; the America that is not afraid, the America that will defend to the end: freedom, equal opportunity, justice, democracy, hard work. Aren't these the principles that forged this nation, built by successive waves of migrants from all over seeking refuge, freedom and a better future? Isn't the story of America one of integration, inclusion, and mutual enrichment?

It is this awareness that allows us to understand that the real challenge is not the arrival of newcomers, but America's ability to remain true to its values. What threatens America today is not the immigrant knocking at its door, but the immigrant who is not American.

It's not the "fear and rejection" of what it is supposed to defend: a land of welcome, a nation strong in its diversity.

In reality, America will not lose its values; I have faith in this nation. What it risks losing is its humanity, its ability to welcome others, to reach out to those fleeing misery, war, and persecution. When America turns in on itself, when it builds walls instead of bridges, that's when these executioners of freedom betray what America truly stands for.

American values are not static. They have evolved over time, with each generation, with each new wave of immigrants who have helped shape this nation. The courage of the pioneers who crossed unknown lands is not so different from that of the men, women, and children who cross borders today in search of a better life.

Yes, immigration can be challenging. Integration requires effort, adaptation, and compromise. But these challenges should not be seen as threats. They are an opportunity to renew and strengthen what makes the United States of America an exceptional nation. By embracing diversity, by opening itself to others, America cannot only preserve its values but revitalize them.

It is this awareness that makes us realize that Springfield is a unique opportunity for us, the Haitians, to better organize ourselves, to take our country's destiny into our own hands, and to succeed in the SHEXIT, but also an opportunity for our two nations to review our shared commitments to freedom, family, dignity and justice. In a world that

is now defined, freedom for us Haitians means staying at home, working to restore our democracy and rebuild our economy as a sovereign nation. Let this last wave of "humanitarian parole" be that of the last immigrants of the precarious generation; freedom means the rebirth of the world's first republic, the second independent country of the Americas, so that the next immigrants from Haiti will be of the proud generation. Those who will visit America, not because Haiti makes them flee, but because they will come to tell Americans what a great pastor said on the steps of the Lincoln Memorial: "Free at last, free at last, thank God Almighty, we are free at last".

People of Haiti, my beloved people,

Since there will be no better world without a better Haiti, Americans cannot continue to disrespect us. We have earned the right to immigrate here and to all the countries where our blood has been shed. So, we have the right to warn America: when a nation loses its fundamental values, its bearings, it goes astray; we know the misfortunes that befall it. We may not be the best advisors on democracy, technology, development, etc., but we know the route. Since we always need someone smaller than ourselves, we will always be that friend who tries to keep America from going astray; just as we need a friend who teaches us how to be great, even though our history with America is full of treachery, infantilism, and disrespect.

Our ancestors have always succeeded here; some gave their lives for freedom, a   others founded one of the greatest cities in the United States. From here, our relatives and friends have contributed to our lives in Haiti. From here we proudly prove that we are hard workers; we are in the streets, we are in the airports, in the hotels, in the hospitals, in the courts; we are in the universities, in the schools that shape America's future; we are in Congress as well as in the White House. Just as there are executioners of freedom in our country, the American people are not spared. Let's reassure them that the liberation of our people is near, but let's also assume that we can continue our friendship, but in a different way; let's assume our challenges of organizing, systematizing, and restoring our democracy, so that without wasting time we can fulfill the legend: Rise from the ashes!

Alexandre Telfort Fils

Each of us has a story to share with our descendants. What's yours? So that our children and grandchildren know the sacrifices we immigrants have made.

_____

_____

_____

_____

_____

_____

_____

_____

_____

_____

_____

_____

_____

_____

_____

_____

_____

_____

_____

_____

_____

_____

_____

BIBLIOGRAPHY

Immigration is a vast and complex subject that has given rise to an abundance of literature, poignant testimonials and detailed reports. To gain an in-depth understanding of immigration issues, it is essential to refer to academic works, historical accounts and studies by specialized organizations. Here is a selection of resources that shed light on the various dimensions of the migration phenomenon in the United States.

A. – Books and articles on immigration to the United States

1. – Academic works

"The Age of Migration: International Population Movements in the Modern World" by Stephen Castles, Hein de Haas and Mark J. Miller (2019)

This book is an essential reference for understanding global migration dynamics. The authors examine the economic, political and social factors influencing contemporary migration, providing a framework for analyzing immigration to the United States in a global context.

"Immigration and American Popular Culture: An Introduction" by Rachel Lee and William C. J. C. Lee (2016)

This book explores how immigration is represented in American popular culture. The authors analyze stereotypes, media images, and the impact of these representations on public perceptions and migration policies.

"The Immigration Debate: The Legal, Economic, Political, and Social Aspects" by David J. Chuh (2018)

This book provides an overview of the many facets of the immigration debate in the United States. The authors examine the legal, economic, political and social aspects, providing a comprehensive guide to understanding the controversies and challenges associated w i t h immigration.

2. – Academic articles

"Immigration and Economic Growth in the United States: A Review of the Evidence" by George J. Borjas (2020)

This article analyzes the economic contributions of immigrants to the United States, examining historical and recent data to assess their impact on economic growth and the labor market.

"The Politics of Immigration: American Perspectives and Global Issues" by Robert C. Smith and Adrian D. Martínez (2017)

This text explores American migration policy by putting global issues into perspective. It offers a critical analysis of current policies and their impact on international relations.

"Cultural Integration and Social Cohesion: The Role of Immigrants in American Society" by Sandra M. Cruz (2021)

This article looks at the cultural integration of immigrants and their role in social cohesion in the United States, highlighting the challenges and successes faced by immigrant communities.

B. – Testimonies and stories of immigrants throughout history

1. – Historical testimonies

"The Warmth of Other Suns: The Epic Story of America's Great Migration" by Isabel Wilkerson (2010)

This book traces the migration of African-Americans from the South to the North and West of the United States. Wilkerson offers poignant personal accounts that illustrate the reasons for and impacts of this migration on American society.

"My Life as a Mexican-American: Stories of Migration and Identity" by Juan Gonzales (2015) Gonzales recounts the experiences of Mexican immigrants in the United States, offering insights into their struggle to integrate and their impact on American culture.

"The Namesake" by Jhumpa Lahiri (2003)

Although a novel, it is based on the real-life experiences of Bengali immigrants in the United States. Lahiri explores themes of identity, belonging and the challenges of dual culture.

2. – Contemporary testimonials

"We Are Here to Stay: Voices of Immigrants and Refugees" by Michael Smith (2021) This collection of contemporary testimonials presents the life stories of immigrants and refugees, offering personal perspectives on the challenges of integration and hopes for the future.

"American Dreams: The Immigrant Experience in Modern America" by Nina L. Gellman (2022)

This book gathers the stories of recent immigrants, offering a glimpse into the contemporary realities and aspirations of newcomers to the United States.

C. – Humanitarian and research reports on the impact of migration policies**.

1. – Reports from humanitarian organizations

"Global Trends: Forced Displacement in 2022" by the United Nations High Commissioner for Refugees (UNHCR)

This report provides detailed data on the situation of refugees and displaced persons worldwide, with insights into migration policies and their impact on vulnerable populations.

"The Impact of Immigration Policies on Refugees and Asylum Seekers in the United States" by Amnesty International (2021)

This report analyzes the effects of U.S. migration policies on refugees and asylum seekers, highlighting the challenges faced by these groups and recommendations for improving policies.

2. – Research reports

"Economic Impact of Immigration: A Study of the U.S. Labor Market" by the National Bureau of Economic Research (NBER) (2022)

This report examines the economic impact of immigration on the U.S. labor market, using empirical data to assess the effects on wages, employment, and productivity.

"Social Integration and Immigrant Communities: Evidence from the United States" by the Migration Policy Institute (MPI) (2023)

This report explores the dynamics of immigrant social integration in the United States, assessing the successes and challenges encountered in integrating immigrant communities.

"The Role of Immigration in American Innovation: Contributions and Challenges" by the Center for American Progress (CAP) (2022)

This report examines how immigrants contribute to innovation and technological growth in the United States, while discussing policies that could support these contributions while addressing the challenges.

The bibliography and sources provided offer a solid foundation for a thorough understanding of immigration to the United States. Academic works, personal testimonials, and reports from humanitarian and research organizations provide a comprehensive overview of the various aspects of immigration. These resources are essential for grasping the complexities of the immigration debate and formulating balanced policies that respect both the rights of immigrants and the interests of host societies. By integrating these perspectives into the discourse on immigration, we can hope to build a future where the values of freedom, equality and solidarity are truly realized.

3. – Other sources

Alami, Aida. 2018. Between Hate, Hope, and Help: Haitians in the Dominican Republic. The New York Review of Books, August 13, 2018. Available online.

Casey, Matthew. 2017. Empire Guest Workers; Haitian Migrants in Cuba during the Age of U.S. Occupation. Cambridge, UK: Cambridge University Press.

Ferrer, Ada. 2012. Haiti, Free Soil, and Antislavery in the Revolutionary Atlantic. American Historical Review, volume 117, no.1 (February): 40-66. Available online.

Foner, Eric. 2010. The Fiery Trial; Abraham Lincoln and American Slavery. New York: W.W. Norton & Company.

Fisher, Sybille. 2013. Bolivar in Haiti: Republicanism in the Revolutionary Atlantic. In Haiti and the Americas, eds. Carla Calargé, Raphael Dalleo, Luis Duno-Gottberg, and Clevis Headley. Jackson, MS: University of Mississippi Press.

Fouron, Georges. 2010. The History of Haiti in Brief. In The Haitian Creole Language: History, Structure, Use, and Education, eds. Arthur K. Spears and Carole M. Berotte Joseph. New York: Rowan & Littlefield Publishers.

Freedom's Journal. 1827. Vol. 1, no 1. Available online.

Glick Schiller, Nina and Georges Eugene Fouron. 2001. Georges Woke up Laughing: Long Distance Nationalism and the Search for Home. Durham, NC: Duke University Press.

Griggs, Earl Leslie and Clifford Prator. 1968. Henry Christophe and Thomas Clarkson, A Correspondence. New York: Greenwood Press.

Heinl, Robert Debs and Nancy Gordon Heinl. 1996. Written in Blood: The Story of the Haitian People, 1492-1995. Lanham, NY: University Press of America.

Holly, Theodore. 1857. Vindication of the Capacity of the Negro Race for SelfGovernance and Civilized Progress as Demonstrated by Historical Events of the Haytian Revolution: and the Subsequent Acts of that Peoples since their National

Independence. New Haven, CT: William

H. Stanley, Printer.

International Organization for Migration (IOM) Haiti. 2016. Border Monitoring SitRep: 29th December 2016. Available online.

Louis Jr., Bertin. 2019. Haitian Migrants Face Deportation and Stigma in HurricaneRavaged Bahamas. The Conversation, December 3, 2019. Available online.

Kavroulaki, Mariana. 2010. The First Nation that Recognized the Greek Independence: Haiti. History of Greek Food blog, January 15, 2010. Available online.

Madiou, Thomas. 1847. Histoire d'Haïti, Volume III. Port-au-Prince: Imprimerie Henri Deschamps.

McKivigan, John R. 2008. Forgotten Firebrand; James Redpath and the Making of Nineteenth-Century America. Ithaca, NY: Cornell University Press.

Montague, Ludwell Lee. 1940. Haiti and the United States. Durham, NC: Duke University Press. Nicolay, John G. and John Hay. 1909. Abraham Lincoln, a History, Volume 6. New York: The Century Co.

Plummer, Brenda Gayle. 1988. Haiti and the Great Powers: 1902-1915. Baton Rouge, LA: Louisiana State University Press.

Reed, Keturah T. 2016. Dominican Republic Violates International Law in Cancelling Citizenship. North Carolina Journal of International Law, January 26, 2016.

Schmidt, Hans. 1971. The United States Occupation of Haiti, 1915-1934. New Brunswick, NJ: Rutgers University Press.

Trouillot, Michel-Rolph. 1990. Haiti: State Against Nation; The Origins and Legacy of Duvalierism. New York: Monthly Review Press.

United States Literary Gazette. 1824. United States Literary Gazette, September 1, 1824. Boston: Cummings, Hilliard, & Co. Available online.

Trouillot, Michel-Rolph. 1995. Silencing the Past; Power and the Production of History.

Boston, MA: The Beacon Press.

UN High Commissioner for Refugees (UNHCR). 2016. Global Trends: Forced

Displacement in 2015. Geneva: UNHCR. Available online.

World Bank. 2020. Annual Remittances Data, updated as of April 2020. Available online.

Wucker, Michelle. 2015. The Dominican Republic's Shameful Deportation Legacy. Foreign Policy, October 8, 2015. Available online.
https://www.migrationpolicy.org/article/haiti-painful-evolution -promised-land-migrantsending-nation
https://www.miamiandbeaches.fr/activités/histoire-et-héritage/lemon-city-et-little-haiti

Printed completed
November 2024

Made in the USA
Columbia, SC
08 February 2025

52958594R00090